ROUTLEDGE LIBRARY EDITIONS:
DEVELOPMENT

PATTERNS OF CARIBBEAN DEVELOPMENT

PATTERNS OF CARIBBEAN DEVELOPMENT

An Interpretive Essay on Economic Change

JAY R. MANDLE

Volume 46

Routledge
Taylor & Francis Group
LONDON AND NEW YORK

First published in 1982

This edition first published in 2011
by Routledge
2 Park Square, Milton Park, Abingdon, Oxon, OX14 4RN

Simultaneously published in the USA and Canada
by Routledge
711 Third Avenue, New York, NY 10017

Routledge is an imprint of the Taylor & Francis Group, an informa business

First issued in paperback 2013

British Library Cataloguing in Publication Data
A catalogue record for this book is available from the British Library

ISBN 13: 978-0-415-58414-2 (Set)
eISBN 13: 978-0-203-84035-1 (Set)
ISBN 13: 978-0-415-59366-3 (hardback)
eISBN 13: 978-0-203-83843-3 (Volume 46)
ISBN 13: 978-0-415-84913-5 (paperback)

Publisher's Note
The publisher has gone to great lengths to ensure the quality of this reprint but points out that some imperfections in the original copies may be apparent.

Disclaimer
The publisher has made every effort to trace copyright holders and welcomes correspondence from those they have been unable to contact.

PATTERNS OF CARIBBEAN DEVELOPMENT
An Interpretive Essay on Economic Change

Jay R. Mandle
Temple University

GORDON AND BREACH SCIENCE PUBLISHERS
New York London Paris

Gordon and Breach, Science Publishers, Inc.
One Park Avenue
New York, NY 10016

Gordon and Breach Science Publishers Ltd.
42 William IV Street
London, WC2N 4DE

Gordon & Breach
58, rue Lhomond
75005 Paris

Library of Congress Cataloging in Publication Data

Mandle, Jay R.
Patterns of Caribbean development.

(Caribbean studies, ISSN 0275-5793 ; v. 2)
1. Caribbean area–Economic conditions–1945-
I. Title. II. Series.
HC151.M35 1982 330.9182'1 82-12022
ISBN 0-677-06000-9

ISBN 0 677 06000-4 ISSN 0275-5793.

To Iz – Teacher, Activist, Friend

Contents

List of Tables

Introduction to the Series

The purpose of this series is to provide a forum in which the major themes and trends affecting the entire region will be explored in depth. Thus, while the island-specific approach is not eschewed, the aim is to develop perspectives on problem-solving in the area as an entirety, both on the local level and in the international context. Hence the emphasis is on the qualitative and quantitative interpretation of the economic and political culture in which the modern Caribbean operates. Historical, demographical and sociological issues, when relevant to the central focus of the series, will also be examined.

Caribbean Studies will publish the research of academic scholars working within the region, as well as Caribbeanists working internationally. Simultaneously, it is anticipated that the monographs will function as a reference data source for libraries, foundations and government agencies with an interest in the Caribbean either exclusively or peripherally.

It is the coeditors' hope that the series will not only launch comprehensive Caribbean studies internationally, but that it will similarly stimulate innovative research and the development of methodology suitable to comparative perspectives. Only when the Caribbean is evaluated in its broadest panorama can the true global importance of the region be appreciated.

Manuscripts may be sent to either of the two coeditors (who will be assisted by an advisory board to be selected from internationally recognized scholars).

Chapter 1

Introduction

This essay is an effort to analyze the present, in the Caribbean, as history. It is an attempt to appraise, against the background of the past, current efforts to overcome the region's legacy of underdevelopment. It poses, in short, for this region, the questions asked more generally by Richard A. Easterlin: "Why isn't the whole world developed?" . . . *will* the whole world become developed? If so, how soon?[1]

Two assumptions underlie this analysis. The first is that contemporary events can only be understood as the outcome and continuation of the historical past. Present developments, as well as those of the future, are governed by a society's previous experience. In the present context, this means that contemporary efforts to achieve economic development cannot be understood without first examining the relative failure of the growth process in the past. But even more importantly the historical experiences of the Caribbean people decisively influence the array of responses that are possible in addressing the problem of development. The culture, skills, and capital endowments which shape contemporary development efforts are present only to the extent they were created in the past. Thus the present-day trajectory of society, as well as the range of options which are realistically feasible for a society, can only be defined when the present is viewed as being intimately interwoven with the past.

The second assumption is that in such a study there is a need to make explicit the framework of analysis which is employed. In the present case what this calls for is, first, a clear definition of the phrase economic development. Issues related to this definitional problem are discussed in the first two chapters. Once defined, development becomes the object of the study, the dependent variable, and the problem of analysis becomes one of specifying the factors which accounted for the only limited extent to which secular or long-term growth was achieved in the region. To do this it is necessary to identify the potential explanatory variables which might have played a role in this process and then proceed to choose among them on the basis of which ones most clearly are important in this region.

It is in the choosing of potential independent variables for closer scrutiny that the role of theory is critical. For the role of theory precisely is to hypothesize causal relations. Theory in this sense becomes a guide to empirical study allowing the investigator to choose only a selected few from the myriad of possible independent variables for close empirical examination. In this study a modified Marxian framework constitutes the basis upon which the selection process is made. The core principle of Marxism which is adopted here is that the relationship of classes in society constitutes a principal dynamic both in defining a society and in identifying patterns of social change.

In its choice of theory this essay differs markedly from the bulk of the economic history currently written in the United States. This difference, however, does not stem from any disagreement concerning the need for theory itself. Indeed the "New Economic History" which currently dominates the field emerged in response to the essentially atheoretical history which dominated the discipline before the mid 1960's. Rather, the difference centers on the contrasting paradigms which are called upon.

The "New Economic History" employes one or another varient of neo-classical, especially, price theory. That is, its focus centers on market relations and analyses. Its efforts therefore lie, essentially, in two realms. It may for example start with an assumption that markets are at equilibrium and attempt to discern how a change in a relevant variable might alter the original equilibria. In this case the importance of the changed independent variable may be measured by estimating the magnitude of the change which results in the equilibrium condition. Alternatively, again using the same neo-classical approach, efforts can be made to measure real world divergences from a theoretical optimum. Here measurements of waste and inefficiency can be made by assuming the markets solutions to the problems of resource allocation are efficient and then comparing the real world to that. In this way, social institutions might be identified as either having contributed to a desirable allocation of resources or might be assigned responsibility for producing an inefficient or sub-optimal allocation of resources.

There are a vast number of historical problems for which the application of neo-classical price theory is useful. The outpouring of historical research which has occurred in the last fifteen years is testimony to that fact.[2] Most economic historians would agree, however, that the neo-classical framework is not appropriate for all the problems in economic history. In particular, the argument presented here is that the problem of development, the secular rise in output, is one of those areas which is not served well by contemporary economic theory. Market theory does not speak effectively to the long-term social mastery of technological innovation which, as we shall see, is the key to economic development. In light of this it is not surprising that neither the long-term growth process nor the stagnation in development in the underdeveloped countries has been high on the agenda of the "new economic historians." Easterlin has put it this way: "the questions which now dominate the study of economic history" do not typically address "the startling contrasts in national experience" with regard to development.[3]

The argument presented here is that, in contrast, Marxist theory is a potentially valuable tool in addressing the long-term growth of society. This, after all, was exactly the question to which Marx addressed himself: the transformation of society and in particular the emergence of socialism out of an industrially mature capitalist economy. Indeed a considerable amount of Marx's effort was to demonstrate the growth-promoting propensities of capitalism. At the same time, though much more briefly, Marx also discussed how non-capitalist social organizations, such as the Asiatic mode of production acted to inhibit the expansion of a society's productive capacity. It is in this context, then, that this study proceeds in Chapter 1–2. The essential theoretical point of departure is a consideration of how specific social organizations and class structures effected the Caribbean's growth process in the past and how they continue to influence present day efforts to promote expansion. In doing so, however, the argument is that it is necessary to identify a mode of production which corresponds closely to the society under investigation and that may well mean identifying forms of social organization different than those discussed by Marx himself.

In a discussion of the historic failure of economic development the English-speaking Caribbean can be treated as a single unit. The various territories of the region were endowed with similar social structures and subjected to the same externally imposed political constraints in the form of colonialism. As a result, despite differences that did exist among them, they shared, fundamentally the same growth pattern. Thus following the lead of George Beckford the framework of the planation economy is employed in Chapter 3 on a region-wide basis to account for the limited extent to which the area experienced development. Similarly the initial effort consciously to stimulate industrialization in the post-World War II years is treated here on a regional basis in Chapter 4. Efforts at "industrialization through invitation" or what is now called "dependent development" were articulated for the region as a whole and implemented on a sufficiently similar manner by many of the territories to make individual island studies unnecessary.

As we shall argue these efforts at externally propelled growth were not without some degree of success. An essentially imported development process was experienced, especially in the larger islands of the region, Jamaica and Trinidad and Tobago. Indeed, this approach to growth continues to dominate in Barbados and the smaller islands of the Eastern Caribbean. But generally the 1950's mode of development was found wanting and gave rise to the demand for an alternative approach to growth. The search was for a model of development which at once would reduce the degree to which external forces and initiatives determined the fate of the region and at the same time would more widely and evenly distribute the benefits of growth than was the case with dependency.

The emerging dissatisfaction with dependent development was linked in the 1960's to the achieving of political independence by the major countries in the region a phenomenon discussed in Chapter 5. From that point forward treating the West Indies as a homogeneous unit for purposes of analysis becomes less and less satisfactory. Increasingly each of the nations of the region in the 1960's and 1970's attempted to fashion its own idiosyncratic solution to its problems. Especially with the crystallization, on a governmental level, of "Left" ideological trends in Jamaica and Guyana and the windfall of petro-dollars in Trinidad and Tobago, directions of change became increasingly divergent. It is for these reasons that in dealing with contemporary efforts at growth the analysis shifts from a regional one to a consideration of individual country experiences in sequential chapters.

It is also in this connection that an examination of Cuba suggests itself. For where the strategy adopted emphasized socialism and autonomy, as was the case in Jamaica and Guyana, the experience of that Spanish-speaking island was obviously relevent. Especially, as we shall see, Cuba's agrarian reform is instructive with regard to the problems which can be anticipated in attempting to achieve agricultural modernization. Consequently a brief examination of that country's agrarian reform is presented, though it should be emphasized that this by no means represents a comprehensive discussion of the Cuban Revolution.

The case studies presented of the 1970's in Jamaica, Guyana and Trinidad and Tobago represent an exploration of the alternative development promoting schemes which have been tried to date in the region. The effort is to analyze the strategies which have been adopted and assess the likelihood that they will be able to achieve a greater degree of growth, autonomy and equity than was achieved during the 1950's and 1960's.

The three countries individually studied here are in terms of population and geographic size the most important in the English-speaking Caribbean. In that sense the discussion concerns the experience of the "typical" West Indian. Thus, of the 4.6 million people resident in nations of the Caribbean Common Market (Caricom) Jamaica's 2 million, Trinidad and Tobago's 1 million and Guyana's 3/4 of a million represent more than 80% of the people living in the English-speaking Caribbean (Table 1.1). It is similarly the case that geographically Guyana, Trinidad and Tobago and Jamaica are the largest of the Caricom nations. Combined, these nations contain almost 90% of the square milage of that grouping of nations. Of course this statistic

Table 1.1

POPULATION AND LAND AREA OF CARICOM COUNTRIES

	1974 Population	Land Area (Sq. Miles)
Jamaica	2,017,191	4,410
Trinidad and Tobago	985,878	1,980
Guyana	768,242	83,000
Three countries combined	3,771,311	99,390
Caricom Total	4,638,131	99,546

Revised and calculated from the source: Sidney Chernick, *The Commonwealth Caribbean*. The Integration Experience A World Bank Country Economic Report (Baltimore and London: The Johns Hopkins University Press, 1978), p. 57.

is misleading since as much as 70,000 of Guyana's 83,000 square miles is forest covered and is either only sparsely or not at all populated. Moreover, more than 90% of Guyana's population is resident on the country's coastal plain. This region, extending from the Essequibo to the Courentyne extends about 100 miles in length and from 2 to 8 miles in width. If for purposes of comparison Guyana were confined only to the coastal plain it thus would still be among the larger of the nations of the region.

Guyana and Trinidad and Tobago do however differ significantly from the rest of the region with regard to the ethnic composition of their respective populations. This is because in the aftermath of Emancipation in 1838 both of these countries replaced their plantation slave labor force with indentured immigrants, to a greater extent than the rest of the region. The bulk of the immigrants came from India, though small numbers came from Africa, China, and Portugal. As a result the ethnic composition of these two countries is much more cosmopolitan and diverse than other countries. In both, the East Indian sub-group is now the largest single component of the total population. Macpherson considers Trinidad's population to be "perhaps the most mixed of all West Indian islands.[4] Elsewhere, as in Jamaica, the composition or of the population is more homogeneous, dominated by descendents of the black slave population.

The conclusions which are reached in this study are not generally optimistic. Trinidad and Tobago's petro-growth has produced vastly expanded levels of income, but there are grounds for grave doubts that this wealth will be employed efficiently to expand the country's ability to produce goods and services and thus experience economic development. At the same time neither of the non revolutionary "Left" regimes in the region, Jamaica and Guyana, were able to harness their economies successfully and thus stimulate growth. In both countries this failure ultimately can be traced to the narrow, specifically non-rural, base of support upon which Michael Manley's administration and Forbes Burnham's regime rested. But the Cuban case illustrates the fact that even the resolution of this political problem by including the countryside in a regime's base of support is no guarantee of success in promoting development. For though the Cuban Revolution does have roots in the countryside, Cuba still has not been able to achieve a sustained expansion in agricultural production. Here the problem seems to be ideological and institutional; that is, finding a match behind the institutional requirements of growth and ideological acceptability.

Of these case studies, the Cuban Revolution seems to provide the best source of hope. The post-Manley government in Jamaica is intent on restoring the strategy of dependent development, seemingly oblivious to the inevitable development-inhibiting tensions and strains associated with that strategy. Guyana's narrowly based government continues to be immobilized by its inability to call upon the trust and good will of the Guyanese people. Trinidad and Tobago, in the post-Williams era seems no more likely to allocate its wealth carefully and bring to fruition feasible projects important in stimulating production than it did in the past. It is only the Cubans who, in the late 1970's and early 1980's have begun seriously to address their development problems. There, efforts have been begun to adjust institutions to the needs of production. Especially in introducing market mechanisms and cooperative production units the Cubans seem to be moving to an institutional and ideological mix which may well be growth-promoting. The Cuban Revolution has not yet attained that goal. But in Cuba, in contrast to the other countries examined here, many of the pre-requisites of growth are already in place and expansion awaits only clear-headed and goal-oriented policy adjustments by the political leadership. How soon and if those goals will be achieved remains to be seen.

NOTES

1. Richard A. Easterlin, "Why Isn't The Whole World Developed?", Presidential address to the Economic History Association, Boston, Mass., Sept. 12, 1980, *The Journal of Economic History* Vol. XLI, No. 1 March, 1981, p. 2, emphasis in original.
2. This work regularly appears in *The Journal of Economic History* and *Explorations in Economic History*.
3. Richard A. Easterlin, "Why Isn't The Whole World Developed?" p. 2.
4. John Macpherson, *Caribbean Lands: A Geography of the West Indies* (Trinidad and Jamaica: Longman Caribbean, Third Edition, 1973), p. 69.

Chapter 2

Marxism and Economic Development

The process of economic development centers on the application of scientific, engineering and technological knowledge to production. Simon Kuznets, the leading empirical student of the development experience, writes that the "mass application of technological innovation . . . constitutes much of the distinctive substance of modern economic growth."[1] Countries which have become developed, according to Kuznets, are the ones which have managed to take advantage of the potential of modern technology. Where this potential has been tapped the characteristics of development too have appeared: population growth has occurred, per capita income increased, the range of production widened, the industrial and occupation structure of the labor force shifted away from blue-collar, and agricultural work and productivity increased. In this context, therefore, underdevelopment is seen as the failure to apply modern technology to production. For the poor countries of the world, underdevelopment is caused by their failure to utilize modern technology extensively while their future economic advance is contingent upon their ability to utilize such production methods.

Modern economic growth, defined in this way, closely corresponds to what Marx referred to as an expansion in the forces of production. Thus after reviewing Marx's use of the phrase forces of production, G. A. Cohen concludes that for Marx:

> The development of scientific knowledge is . . . the centre of the development of the productive forces. In its higher stages the development of the productive forces . . . merges with the development of productively useful science.[2]

The forces of production themselves include labor power, raw materials, tools, machines and other materials. The level of development of the forces of production is represented by the productivity of these "inputs" in production. As Marx himself put it "the growth of the productive forces of labour means merely that less direct labour is required in order to make a larger product."[3] Thus when Kuznets refers to "modern economic growth" it is safe to assume that he is discussing what Marx, a century earlier, discussed as an advance in the forces of production.

But the similarities in approach between Kuznets and Marx do not end with this definitional agreement. There is, in addition, agreement with regard to the sources of the process of expansion. Both are committed to the view that the causes of growth are to be found in the structure of society. In the Marxian paradigm it is the society's relations of production, broadly its class structure, which plays a causal role in the development of the productive forces; furthermore it is argued that the class structure of some kinds of societies are more conducive to economic development than others.

Kuznets generally corroborates this view, though his discussion of the "noneconomic" determinants of growth is less specific than Marx's. Kuznets' formal definition of development is ". . . a long-term rise in capacity to supply increasingly diverse economic goods . . . this growing capacity based on advancing technology and the institutional and ideological adjustments it demands." He goes out of his way, however, to emphasize that all three components of his definition – technology, institutions and ideology – are important. Indeed he argues that "if advancing technology is to be employed efficiently and widely, and, indeed, if its own progress is to be stimulated by such use, institutional and ideological adjustments must be made to effect the proper use of innovations generated by the advancing stock of human knowledge."[4] In this view technological change is the proximate source of economic development, but its rate of advance is itself the consequence of the institutional configuration and dominant ideology of the country in question. Formulated analytically, technology change can be seen as the dependent variable whose level and rate of change is influenced by the independent variables, institutions and ideologies, again a position fully consistent with the Marxian approach.

Marx, according to Avineri, believed that

> ... what ultimately gave rise to the bourgeois world and industrialization was the slow differentiation of a sphere of activity which legitimized profit-oriented economic activity as an autonomous field, no more encumbered by the ethical religious and political restrictions of the feudal order.[5]

In this autonomous sphere – or civil society – only economic criteria of profitability and efficiency govern behavior. In this context competition between firms, each of which attempts to maximize profits, serves as the mechanism by which scientific and technological advances are applied to production. In the meantime the separation of most of the population from land ownership means that new industries are able to recruit workers and supply themselves with a labor force. In combination these three – a culture which authenticates profit-maximizing behavior, a mobile labor force and competition among firms – are the critical growth-promoting characteristics of capitalism. Capitalist culture allows for the unrestricted introduction of new methods of production, competition speeds this process and labor mobility facilitates the emergence of new, technologically advanced sectors of economic activity. In the *Grundrisse* Marx wrote that "development of the productive forces of social labour is the historical task and justification of capital." This view was even more clearly expressed in *The Communist Manifesto* where Marx and Engels wrote that the "constant revolutionizing of production, uninterrupted disturbance of all social conditions, everlasting uncertainty and agitation distinguish the bourgeois epoch from all earlier ones."[6]

But Marx believed more than merely that where capitalism was present development would occur. He also believed that capitalism itself would spread throughout the world. Capitalism, wrote Marx and Engels, "compels all nations, on pain of extinction, to adopt the bourgeois mode of production; it compels them to introduce what it calls civilization into their midst, i.e., to become bourgeois themselves. In a word it creates a world after its own image." In *Capital* Marx acknowledges that he treats "the whole world as one nation and assumes that capitalist production is everywhere established and has possessed itself of every branch of industry." In short Marx believed that "the country that is more developed industrially only shows to the less developed the image of its own future."[7]

Especially with regard to Asia, Marx was quite explicit concerning the growth promoting characteristics of capitalism. He argued that the imposition of colonial rule from abroad set the stage of the installing of capitalism and for a decisive advance in the forces of production. In an article entitled, "The Future Results of British Rule in India," published in 1853, Marx argued that with British investment in railroads, economic development in the subcontinent would be triggered. He wrote that

> . . . when you have once introduced machinery into the locomotion of a country which possesses iron and coal, you are unable to withhold it from its fabrication. . . . The railway system will therefore become, in India, the forerunner of modern industry.

In short, according to Marx, "England has to fulfill a double mission in India: one destructive, the other regenerating – the annihilation of the old Asiatic society and the laying of material foundations of Western society in Asia."[8] Marx, in short, as Kiernan has written, anticipated that colonialism would not only lead to the industrialization of India by the British, "but he was hopeful of something even better, industrialization by Indian enterprise."[9]

In retrospect, it is clear however that Marx was excessively optimistic with regard to the spread of economic development. The diffusion of economic development did not occur as rapidly or extensively as he believed it would. Paul Bairoch's estimates of per capita product, for example, reveal that for at least a half century after Marx wrote, the spread of economic development which he anticipated failed to occur. It is not until the years after World War II that the kind of rapid expansion in output which Marx expected actually occurred in the "third world." (See Table 2.1.) At best, therefore, Marx was premature in his views concerning the spread of development.

The same general conclusion can be inferred from contemporary growth rate data. (See Table 2.2.) Thus, the World Bank reports an average of 1.4 percent per year for recent years for the 37 poorest countries in the world for which data are available. Though this rate is below that of higher income countries, it is nonetheless clear that this experience is in excess of the expansion which must have occurred in years prior to

Table 2.1

GROSS NATIONAL PRODUCT PER CAPITA, 1750–1977, BY REGION
(1960 US dollars and prices)

Year	Developed Countries	Third World
1750	182	188
1800	198	188
1830	237	183
1860	324	174
1880	406	176
1900	540	175
1913	662	192
1928	781	194
1938	856	202
1950	1054	203
1960	1453	250
1970	2229	308
1977[a]	2739	355

[a] Provisional figures

Source: P. Bairoch, "Income Inequalities among Nations before the Industrial Revolution and their Evolution till the 1970's," in P. Bairoch and M. Levy-Leboyer, ed., *Regional and International Disparities in Economic Development since the Industrial Revolution* (London: Macmillan, 1981), Table 3.

Table 2.2

AVERAGE ANNUAL RATE OF GROWTH OF GNP PER CAPITA BY INCOME LEVEL, 1960–1978

Low Income (37)	1.6
Middle Income (55)	3.7
Industrialized (18)	3.7
Centrally Planned (17)	4.0

Revised and calculated from the source: The World Bank, *World Development Report 1980*, pp. 110–111.

1960. For these are countries whose per capita output range between $80 (US) and $300 (US) and in 25 of which GNP per capita is $200 (US) or less. From such levels we can infer that historically they could not have experienced positive growth rates over an extended period of time in the past. Assuming the existence of some irreducibly low level, it follows that if current growth rates had existed in the past, present-day levels of per capita output would be much higher than they, in fact, are.

The failure of the diffusionist growth mechanism envisioned by Marx calls into question at least one, if not both, of two major Marxian hypotheses. It might mean that capitalism is not everywhere a growth promoting mode of production. Alternatively the failure of the spread of development might suggest that the expansion of capitalism internationally in the nineteenth and early twentieth centuries was less extensive than most Marxist observers believe. In this view underdevelopment would be associated with the persistence of non-bourgeois modes of production. Acceptance of the first would represent a radical revision of the basic Marxist paradigm. Acceptance of the second, while less threatening to the basic Marxist framework, leads to the need to specify carefully the components of capitalism and the need to delineate other noncapitalist modes of production.

Marx himself seems consistently to have held to the second view: where development did not occur, capitalism was not present. But Marx was also aware of the limitations of his work in studying the spread internationally of capitalism and growth. In this regard Avineri cites an 1877 letter by Marx warning his disciples not to "metamorphose my historical sketch of the genesis of capitalism in Western Europe into a historico-philosophic theory of the general path every people is fated to tread." In the same letter Marx goes on to say that "the chapter on primitive accumulation [in Capital] does not pretend to do more than trace the path by which, in Western Europe, the capitalist order of economy emerged from the womb of the Feudal order of society."[10] Furthermore Marx's writings on regions which were to become the Third World are scattered and fragmentary. He paid very little attention to South America and next to none to Africa. Marx did however contribute a substantial literature to events in Asia, especially with regard to British colonial policy in India. It is primarily from these sources that Marx's views on non-European development can be gleaned.

Marx attributed the failure of the forces of production to advance in Asia to that region's mode of production, a mode of production which, he argued, was different from capitalism. In his study *Marx and the Third World*, Umberto Melotti summarizes Marx's views on the Asiatic mode of production. There are three basic features of this model of society, Melotti writes:

> First there is no private ownership of land; in the last resort, at least, it belongs to the State. Second, the base is a system of village communes, each one made self-sufficient through a close combination of agriculture and cottage crafts. Third, the central power plays a commanding role . . .

especially with regard to the demand for water control facilities and other public works.[11] As such it is clear that the Asiatic mode of production is fundamentally different from contemporaneous European modes of production. Especially differences exist with respect to the existence of personal dependency in the European context. Melotti argues "slavery and personal dependence exist in Asia only marginally . . . but [unlike Europe] they never become the fundamental relations of production."[12]

Within the framework of the Asiatic mode of production the scope for advances in the forces of production was minute compared to the explosion in technology which occurred under capitalism. This difference can be traced to the circumstances in which technology flourishes. As we have seen, Marx argued that the major advances in the forces of production can occur only when an increasing sphere of life, and particularly economic activity is freed from politico-religious influences. Such a free space was associated with the increasing importance of private land ownership in Europe. But the absence of individual land ownership and a free market for land in the Asiatic mode of production implied that the scope of unconstrained economic behavior was narrow.[13] According to Sawer, the sources of retardation in Marx's Asiatic mode of production were found on two levels: "Above, the monopolisation of economic initiative and surplus value by a centralized state apparatus; below, the perpetuation of a natural economy in socially isolated, self-sufficient village communities."[14] As a result even if there were a demand for an increased volume of production, the capacity to respond to market opportunities with improved production techniques was severely limited. So too was the capacity to achieve an Asian industrial revolution thus rendered minimal.

So severe was this constraint that it induced an even more profound stagnation than is suggested by the absence of an industrial revolution. Marx found no internally generated means by which the Asiatic mode of production could be transcended. For, unlike the feudalism of Europe in which capitalism grew, precisely the totalitarianism of the Asiatic mode of production stifled such creative stirrings. Not only did the forces of production fail to develop extensively in this setting, but at the same time, the Asiatic mode of production was stagnant over the long-run in the sense that potentially growth promoting modes of production were stillborn under its oppressive hegemony. Potential agents of change were present. But the fact was that groups such as State officials, peasants, landed proprietors, in Melotti's words, "never managed, under a suffocating State power, to gain for any length of time that degree of social and political power ideological and cultural freedom that in the West opened the way to capitalism."[15] Sawer makes the same point: "For Marx the East was stagnant because the state, with its monopoly of surplus value, prevented the growth of competing economic classes."[16] The Asiatic mode of production thus had strong self-reinforcing characteristics. It was with this in mind that Marx wrote of it that "civil wars, invasions, revolutions, conquests, famines . . . did not go deeper than its surface. . . ."[17] The logic of this discussion is that since advances in the forces of production of an extensive scale were not possible within the Asiatic mode of production and revolutionary advances from that mode of production were unlikely, economic growth in Asia awaited external intervention.

It is thus clear that Marx in writing about Asia took seriously his own injunction concerning the limited applicability of his major writings. The framework of analysis which he sketched for the study of India and China differed very considerably from the approach taken with regard to Europe. In the first place Marx's model of Asian society – the Asiatic mode of production – was completely dissimilar from any mode of production which he had suggested with regard to the European experience. Furthermore, there is, in Marx's work, no hint that the Asiatic mode of production would ever transform itself into feudalism or capitalism. Third, unlike anything which he wrote about European-based modes of production, Marx identified no dynamic internal to the Asiatic mode of production. Thus not only did this new model of society not fit conveniently into the stages of history sequence Marx sketched for Europe, but the historical dynamic found in Europe and which gave rise to the emergence of a new mode of production from an old one was similarly absent. In the Asiatic mode of production Marx saw nothing but stagnation. Logically this had to mean that if change were to come to Asia it would have to be imposed from outside. Marx did not shrink from this inference and his writings on British colonial policy in India were informed by just such a perspective. On one hand Marx was acidic in his condemnation of the motives and methods of British policy in India and yet, at the same time, he pointed to and affirmed the progressive and dynamic implications of these policies.[18]

In short, Marx himself has provided a license for creativity in the study of non-European societies which has too little been used by Marxists. This license exists along at least three dimensions. First, Marxist students of non-European societies need not, in constructing their models of society, be confined to the orthodoxy of the ancient, slave, feudal, capitalist, communist sequence. Other previously unspecified and significantly different models may be of greater utility in the analysis of such societies than the traditional ideal types. Second, the question of the extent to which the relations of production of such societies facilitated and transformed the forces of production should be an open one. Again, following Marx's lead with respect to Asia, it is plausible that only a very limited dynamic might have been present in any particular setting. The third follows from the second. If little or no dynamic were present within a particular mode of production then it follows that Marxists should be willing to entertain the possibility that such dynamism could be induced only through external contact or even intervention. This, of course, is the origin of Marx's dialectical view of colonialism.

Each of these perspectives is important and deserves careful consideration in its own right. Yet it is also important to look at them in combination. For what they suggest is that Marx himself in looking at the societies which were to constitute the underdeveloped world was not locked into the familiar orthodoxy which is described as Marxism. Marx did not find it necessary to squeeze all societies into the traditional sequence; nor was he committed to the view that all societies contain within them the sources of internally induced change or that even colonialism was an unambiguous evil. The issue is not whether Marx was correct in these hypotheses; rather the key point is that Marx was, and therefore, by extension, Marxists ought to be free to consider these heretical viewpoints.

Marx's work on Asia, however, has not been without its critics. Perry Anderson, for example, has condemned the concept of the Asiatic mode of production on both empirical and theoretical grounds. Its characteristics, he argues, fail to correspond to the actual components of Chinese and Islamic civilizations. Furthermore he argues that the concept suffers from "the inherent weakness of functioning essentially as a generic residual category for non-European development, blending features found in distinct social formations into a single blurred archetype." Anderson's view is that insufficient historical research has been carried out to provide the basis for conclusions about the modes of production which prevailed in early modern Asian history.

It is striking, however, that while Anderson suggests that the Asiatic mode of production "be given the decent burial that it deserves," his view concerning the emergence of capitalism and economic development in Asia are not inconsistent with those of Marx. Though he attacks the view that Asian societies were stationary, he does acknowledge "the absence of a feudal dynamic of the Western type in the great Orient Empires." He contends that "very great changes and advances" occurred, though he concedes, as he puts it, that "these did not debauch onto capitalism."[19]

Sawer's view is that Anderson's attempt to bury the Asiatic

mode of production is "ungenerous," for, as she points out, Anderson does accept the basic lesson of the Asiatic mode of production concept for Marxists: "that concepts pertaining to Western European social formations should not be lightly extended to formations found outside the realm of Western Europe historical experience and juridico-political structures."[20] Thus as noted by Sawer, even as severe a critic as Anderson follows Marx's lead in hypothesizing the existence of historical modes of production which at once were different than those which emerged in Europe and in which the process of economic development was largely absent. Implicit in the views of both Anderson and Sawer is the position that carefully constructed modes of production, specifically applicable to discrete regions, should be posited in order to study nonbourgeois social structures.

An example of just such an effort is provided by the work of Catherine Coquery-Vidrovitch in her study of Africa. In dealing with that continent Coquery-Vidrovitch is concerned with a region which, as noted above, Marx scarcely addressed at all. She furthermore explicitly denies that Marx's Asiatic mode of production is relevant to her concern. Instead she hypothesizes the existence of an African mode of production. She writes that

> The only thing that the two systems have in common is the existence of subsistence village communities. In Asia, however, it is a question of despotism and direct exploitation through generalized slavery whereas in Africa . . . there is a superimposed bureaucracy which interferes only indirectly with the community.

The uniqueness of the African social setting rested in the joining of a patriarch-communal economy with the ascendancy of one group over long-distance trade. In these circumstances, she argues, economic development was unlikely to occur both because a sparse population meant that "the necessity of improving production with the aid of new tools or large public works was never felt" and because investment in long-distance trade was "sterile". Under such a regime she argues "the productive forces are not real forces."[21] With a limited population density inhibiting the incentive to innovate and the pattern of investment constraining the capacity to advance productivity, stagnation prevailed in Africa. Thus Coquery-Vidrovitch follows

Marx himself in hypothesizing that the failute of development, in this case in Africa, is attributable to the presence of a non-capitalist mode of production.

There is a paradox in the fact that this viewpoint, illustrated by Coquery-Vidrovitch and faithful to Marx's own writings has been very much a minority position among Marxists in the twentieth century. Rather than searching for the sources of underdevelopment in a non-bourgeois mode of production, most contemporary Marxists find its origins in capitalism itself. The argument is that contemporary capitalism in contrast to that of the past is not or at least is not always a growth promoting mode of production. This position was first fully articulated in 1928 at the Sixth Congress of the Communist International. There, in a discussion of revolutionary movements in colonial and semi-colonial countries, a distinction was drawn between

> . . . those colonies which have served the capitalist countries as colonizing regions for their surplus population and which in this way have become extensions of the capitalist system (Australia, Canada, etc.), and those which are exploited by the imperialists primarily as markets for their commodities, as sources of raw materials and as spheres for capital investment.

Colonies which have absorbed surplus population became "members of the given imperialist system with equal or nearly equal rights." But in colonies of the second type ". . . the ruling imperialism is related to the colonial countries primarily as a parasite, sucking the blood from the economic organism." To be sure, in this situation there is

> some encouragement of colonial production [but] this is directed on such lines and promoted only in such a degree as corresponded to the interests of the metropolis and in particular to the interests of the preservation of its colonial monopoly.

As a result

> colonial forms of capitalist exploitation . . . hinder the development of the productive forces of the colony. . . . Real industrialization of the colonial country, in particular the building up of a flourishing engineering industry which would promote the independent development of the productive forces, is not encouraged but on the contrary is hindered by the metropolis.[22]

The lag in the economic development of the third world in conjuction with the apparent world-wide spread of capitalism made this revision highly credible. The negative hypothesis concerning capitalism's ability to stimulate development gained wide acceptance among Marxists. Especially during the 1950s and 1960s, when extensive attention was directed to the problems of underdeveloped countries, Marxist opinion was virtually unanimous in agreeing that integration in the world capitalist economy ensured the continued underdevelopment of the "third world." Probably the most sophisticated expression of this view was contained in Paul A. Baran's 1957 publication, *The Political Economy of Growth*. Based largely on the experience of India, Baran's thesis was that imperialism stifled the emergence of an indigenous capitalism.

Preempted by foreign competition from the most lucrative sectors of the economy, the local capitalists according to Baran were prevented from becoming a fully industrialized capitalist class. Faced with the choice of mobilizing a capitalist/worker/peasant alliance to carry through a full bourgeois revolution or accommodating itself to foreign capital, the local business leaders chose the latter course. They did so because in the era of ascendant socialism internationally, the risks were great that the masses, once mobilized, would carry a revolution beyond capitalist limits. The failure to achieve a full bourgeois revolution however meant that the prebourgeois ruling class was permitted to remain intact. Because of their disinterest in productive investment and their propensity for luxury consumption their continued dominance doomed the underdeveloped country to poverty. The social surplus generated would continue to tend not to be used for productive investment. As a result new sources of economic activity would not be created and underdevelopment would persist.[23]

Since Baran's work, such influential Marxist writes as S. Amin, A. Emmanual and A. G. Frank have been in firm agreement that capitalism is unlikely to generate economic development in today's poor countries. It is striking, however, that among such writers the explanation of this failure differs considerably. Amin's work is closest to Baran's. He argues that the penetration of foreign capital results in the formation of "peripheral capitalism," a social formation in which the complete articulation of the capitalist mode of production is blocked and thus economic development is aborted.[24] Emmanuel, however, argues that underdevelopment occurs because of the absence of high wages in the poor country. Low wages produce an insufficiently large market to warrant large volumes of output and the development of a capital goods sector. Though conceding that a high wage policy "could still prove successful in certain cases," Emmanuel goes on to argue that "actually as far as the underdeveloped countries of today are concerned, this road seems to have become impossible in practice." This is because private capitalists today have little interest in promoting such a policy given the existence of already large markets elsewhere.[25] Finally A. G. Frank argues that a transfer of wealth is the key to the "development of underdevelopment." Frank hypothesizes a set of metropolitan/satellitic relationships throughout the world. Once integrated into these market relationships, a country's or region's resources progressively gravitate to the center, thereby preventing development in the hinterland, while the center reaps the benefits of these transfers in the form of development.[26]

Despite the obvious differences among the contemporary Marxists concerning the reasons for the failure of economic development to spread, there is agreement on one central issue: integration into the world capitalist system acts to retard the process of economic development. The mechanism of this retardation vary according to the author. But in all cases the conclusion is the same: contemporary capitalism seen as an integrational system is not a growth promoting mode of production.

What should be noted in all of this is not only that these views are in contrast to those of Marx, but in addition they are not identical either with those expressed at the 1928 meeting of the Communist International. It will be recalled, that the discussion which occurred then was concerned with colonialism and not capitalism. The argument was that in some colonies growth could be anticipated but in others colonial rule inhibited expansion. The position was that it was the external imposition of foreign rule and the policies associated with that rule which prevented the development of the forces of production. Left open was the possibility that, in the absence of the restrictive policies associated with colonialism, capitalist expansion was possible. But it is the denial of the latter in the contemporary world at least which is the basic thrust of much present-day Marxist thought. To the latter the failure of development is systemic, inhering in capitalism itself, and not the product merely of growth-inhibiting policy.

Unfortunately, the process of evaluating this hypothesis has been plagued because of a debilitating weakness which has plagued the Marxist literature on development. Definitional clarity with respect to the content of economic development has not been present. For example, in the case of Frank, one searches in vain for a working definition of either development or underdevelopment. Amin, on the other hand, provides an excessively broad definition of underdevelopment.[27]

The failure to delimit the definition of economic development in this way meant that Marxists in the 1950s and 1960s, hypothesized the continuation of underdevelopment without subjecting their view to empirical verification. Because of this it was not until the 1970s that it was first realized by Marxists that their unambiguously negative view of the prospects for capitalist development was at variance with current experience. Finally, in 1973 Bill Warren published a self-consciously iconoclastic article detailing the industrialization which had occurred in the underdeveloped countries and challenging the dominant Marxist orthodoxy, a challenge which was quickly corroborated by Ian Roxborough and Patrick Clawson among others.[28]

As we have seen there is by now a considerable body of data which supports Warren's position that capitalist development is occurring rapidly in at least some "third world" countries. Indeed the World Bank's data suggests that the "middle income" countries at present are growing at rates which approximate or even exceed those of the industrialized countries. Current growth rates imply a doubling of per capita output in about 25 years. Thus the data strongly suggest that in the post World War II period a process of sustained expansion in the economies of the underdeveloped countries has been initiated.

The conclusion which emerges, then, is that both Marx's original optimistic and subsequent neo-Marxist pessimistic views of capitalist economic development are too facile. The experience between 1800 and 1950 demonstrates that the extension of international trade and capitalist influence is not a sufficient condition for the emergence of economic development. But the experience after World War II also demonstrates that, contrary to the views of the neo-Marxists, neither does capitalist penetration always impede development. The analytic problem which presents itself therefore is two-fold. On one hand it is necessary to specify the mode of production which prevailed in regions in which growth did not occur and to account for this failure. On the other hand it is also necessary for the period in which growth did occur to probe the means by which this expansion was initiated.

NOTES

1. Simon Kuznets, "Modern Economic Growth: Findings and Reflections," in Simon Kuznets, *Population Capital and Growth* (New York: W. W. Norton & Co., 1973), pp. 166, 171.
2. G. A. Cohen, *Karl Marx's Theory of History: A Defense* (Princeton: Princeton University Press, 1978), p. 45.
3. Marx, *Grundrisse*, p. 831, as cited in Cohen, *Karl Marx's Theory of History*, p. 55.
4. Kuznets, "Modern Economic Growth of Findings and Reflections," pp. 165–166.
5. Shlomo Avineri, "Marx and Modernization," *Review of Politics* 31, 2 (April 1969):178.
6. Marx, *Grundrisse* as quoted in Cohen, *Karl Marx's Theory of History*, p. 201, and Marx and Engels, *Manifesto of the Communist Party* as reprinted in Robert Freedman, ed., *Marx on Economics* (New York: Harcourt, Brace & Co., 1961), p. 15.
7. Marx and Engels, *Manifesto of the Communist Party* as reprinted in Freedman, ed., *Marx on Economics*, p. 17; Karl Marx, *Capital Critique of Political Economy* (New York: Modern Library, 1906), pp. 636, 613.
8. Quoted in Avineri, "Marx and Modernization," pp. 132–133.
9. Victor Kiernan, "Marx and India," in Ralph Miliband and John Saville, eds., *The Socialist Register, 1967* (New York: Monthly Review Press, 1967), p. 168.
10. Marx letter to Otechestvenniye Zapiski, in Shlomo Avineri, ed., *Karl Marx on Colonialism and Modernization* (Garden City: Doubleday & Co., 1968), p. 5.
11. Umberto Melotti, *Marx and the Third World* (Atlantic Highlands: Humanities Press, 1977), p. 54.
12. Melotti, *Marx and the Third World*, p. 64.
13. Shlomo Avineri, "Marx and Modernization," *Review of Politics* 31, 2 (April 1969):178, 181–182.
14. Marian Sawer, *Marxism and the Question of the Asiatic Mode of Production* (The Hague: Martinus Nijhoff, 1977), p. 61.
15. Melotti, *Marx and the Third World*, p. 103.
16. Sawer, *Marxism and the Question of the Asiatic Mode of Production*, p. 56.
17. Karl Marx, "The British Rule in India," in Avineri, ed., *Karl Marx on Colonialism and Modernization*, p. 84.

18. Avineri, *Marx on Colonialism and Modernization*, p. 84.
19. Perry Anderson, *Lineages of the Absolutist State* (Atlantic Highlands: Humanities Press, 1974), pp. 494–495.
20. Sawer, *Marxism and the Question of the Asiatic Mode of Production*, p. 231.
21. Catherine Coquery-Vidrovitch, "Research on an African Mode of Production," in Martin A. Klein and G. Wesley Johnson, eds., *Perspectives on the African Past* (Boston: Little, Brown & Co., 1972), pp. 36, 45.
22. "Extracts from the Theses on the Revolutionary Movement in Colonial and Semi-Colonial Countries adopted by the Sixth Comintern Congress," in Jane Degras, ed., *The Communist International 1919–1943 Documents*, II, 1923–1928 (London, New York, Toronto: Oxford University Press, 1960), p. 534.
23. Paul A. Baran, *The Political Economy of Growth* (New York: Monthly Review Press, 1957), pp. 167–248.
24. Samir Amin, *Accumulation on a World Scale*, 2 Vols. (New York: Monthly Review Press, 1974), I, 15.
25. Arghiri Emmanuel, *Unequal Exchange, A Study of the Imperialism of Trade* (New York: Monthly Review Press, 1972), pp. 378–380.
26. Andre Gunder Frank, *Capitalism and Underdevelopment in Latin America*, rev. ed. (New York: Monthly Review Press, 1969).
27. Amin lists three "structural features by which underdevelopment is revealed." These are (1) unevenness of productivity between sectors, (2) disarticulation of the economic system, and (3) domination from abroad. See Amin, *Accumulation on a World Scale*, I, 15.
28. Bill Warren, "Imperialism and Capitalist Industrialization," *New Left Review* 81, September/October 1973; Patrick Clawson, "The Internationalization of Capital Accumulation," *The Insurgent Sociologist*, Spring 1977; Ian Roxborough, "Dependency Theory in the Sociology of Development: Some Theoretical Problems," *Western African Journal of Sociology and Political Science*, Vol. 1, No. 2 (January 1976).

Chapter 3

Economic Development and Human Welfare

Despite his concern with development it is clear that for Marx an advance in the productive forces implied little with regard to living standards. Indeed, the thrust of Marx's critique of capitalism lies precisely in the contrast between the expansion of the capacity to produce and the limited extent to which those benefits will be realized by the population within that system. As he and Engels wrote in *The Communist Manifesto*, "the bourgeoisie, during its rule of scarce one hundred years, has created more massive and modern colossal productive forces than all preceding generations together," but "the modern labourer . . . instead of rising with the progress of industry, sinks deeper and deeper below the conditions of existence of his own class."[1] Thus, in following Marx, an expansion in the forces of production – the process of economic development – can be discussed without assuming that there were positive welfare implications associated with that growth.

Looked at it in this way the phrases "economic development" and "economic growth" can be used interchangeably. In doing this the distinction, currently observed in the literature, between growth and development is deliberately avoided. Frequently growth is used to refer to a narrowly defined process of expanding output, whereas development is reserved for a situation in which that expanding output results in an advance in the welfare of the population. In our usage, however, development and growth are phrases which refer strictly to production and to production methods. Whether and to what extent the benefits of production are widely distributed is an analytically separate and distinct issue from how and at what level production is carried on. Certainly it can be argued that development is a necessary condition for the satisfying of human needs. It is also true that the mechanisms by which output is distributed cannot be entirely separated from the growth process. But the point is that the relationship between growth and distribution is loose and that the influence of one on the other is not predetermined.

In fact the failure of development to be of benefit to large sections of the populations of the poor nations has been reported in a number of papers. In a study prepared for the World Bank Morawetz examined whether a positive relationship existed between economic development, measured by growth rates in per capital output for about sixty capitalist countries between 1960 and 1970 and advances in sixteen measures of basic human needs. The sixteen indicators of basic needs employed by Morawetz covered such essentials as nutrition (3), health (6), housing (3), and education (4).[2]

Morawetz's conclusion is that a statistically significant relationship was found in only five of the sixteen variables. No indication was found at all that with growth there were advances in education. Growth was associated with an increase in the proportion of houses having access to electricity, but there was no such relationship with the average number of persons per room or the percentage of dwellings without piped water. Of the six measures of health examined only the mortality rate for children aged 1–4 was significantly related to development. Unaffected were measures concerned with the availability of hospitals, medical personnel as well as life expectancy at birth and infant mortality rates. It is in the area of nutrition that growth did have an effect, with caloric and protein consumption all positively associated with increasing incomes per capita. Despite this however, Morawetz's conclusion was generally gloomy: "GNP per capita and its growth rate do not seem to provide satisfactory proxies for fulfillment of basic needs and improvements in the same."[3]

In point of fact there has been a remarkable similarity between the economic development process experienced since World War II and that of the 19th century in Europe. Irma Adelman and Cynthia Taft Morris in discussing poverty in the industrial revolution concluded that

> . . . the early stage of economic progress in the first part of the 19th century was usually characterized by unfavorable impacts on the very poor. . . . Rapid population growth, mechanization of production and the impoverishment of small landholders all negatively

> affected the poor and it was only after a considerable lag that these consequences were redressed."

In short, the early industrial revolution failed to improve living standards for the poor of Europe in much the same way that Third World development in the second half of the 20th century has also by-passed large numbers of people. In fact, Adelman and Morris write that their "study suggests that the phenomena generating poverty in 1850 were surprisingly similar to those operating in today's underdeveloped countries, although their range was less wide."[4]

Despite, therefore, or perhaps because the postwar years have seen more rapid growth than in the historical past, development economics among both theorists and policymakers is in disarray. Thus, in calling for a "new economics of the less developed countries" Nake Kamrony and John E. Elliot wrote that

> ... after a quarter century of experimentation with economic development in the poorer countries, the disarray and in some cases calamitous results are so obvious that a fresh look and reexamination of traditional assumptions, methodologies, theories and policies is needed.

They go on to assert that they "do not believe that it is necessary to argue this point at length, since both supporters and critics of the record of economic development of the poor countries agree that reappraisal is necessary."[5] Indeed such a consensus does appear to exist. Such well-established authorities as Benjamin Higgins and Gustav Ranis share it, as does a representative of the World Bank, David Morawetz. In this vein Higgins writes that

> ... disappointment and frustration arose from the wide differences in performance masked by the average rate of growth of LDC's as a whole. ... But there was a still more disturbing element of the experience of the 1960's. Even countries with quite respectable rates of growth of national income did not enjoy "development" in the sense of wide and deep improvement in welfare for the masses of the population. On the contrary unemployment grew, inflation accelerated, the number of malnourished and undernourished people increased, the number of illiterate people also increased, there were more children out of school than in school, health targets were not attained and inequality of income distribution became worse than ever.[6]

Ranis picks up these same themes by arguing that issues such as personal and regional income inequality, unemployment and poverty do not necessarily decline with growth in per capita income but that "these issues are now dominant on the agenda of any political or expert group concerned with development."[7] Generally as Morawetz has put it

> It is now considered that maximization of GNP per capita is too narrow an aim and that other aims related to poverty reduction need to be considered as well: improving income distribution, increasing employment, fulfilling basic needs.[8]

What all of this is suggestive of is something which Marx tried to teach more than a century ago: an advance in the forces of production – the process of economic development – does not necessarily result in the creation of a just or equitable society. The latter is contingent upon the use to which the society's wealth is put – a pattern which is determined by the social relations of production – the class structure. Development under capitalism, according to Marx, "will neither emancipate nor materially mend the social condition of the mass of the people," though it will "lay down the material premises for both." True social advance, according to Marx, depends "not only on the development of the productive power, but on their appropriation by the people."[9]

Implicit in Marx's position is the hypothesis that some patterns of economic development are more exclusionary than others. While it is conceivable that problems with the providing of health, housing, nutrition, and education are inevitably associated with the early stages of economic development, it is also possible, for example, that a socialist system might more readily address these areas than a capitalist system. In short, it is plausible to hypothesize that the mode of production influences the allocation of society's resources so significantly that at comparable levels of development one form of social organization will accomplish significantly more with respect to basic needs than another.

It is precisely this question which Bronco Horvat attempted to examine in a recent study. Horvat, a Yugoslav economist, collected data on three of the four parameters employed in the Morawetz study – life expectancy, education and medical care for sixty countries including ten nations of the socialist bloc.* He then ranked the countries by their level of per capita output. By comparing their per capita output ranking with a composite ranking of social indicators, Horvat was able to judge the relative success a country experienced in satisfying basic needs compared to other countries. Where the basic welfare ranking was lower than the economic development ranking "then the common man is not treated as well as elsewhere." Where, however, the basic welfare ranking is higher than the economic development level, the country is efficiently employing its resources to satisfy the welfare needs of its population.[10]

In fact, Horvat concluded that the countries of the socialist bloc, the countries he characterizes as "etatist," achieved "unambiguously higher basic welfare than other countries."[11] Using 1968 per capita income all but one of the socialist countries possessed a welfare rank in excess of its development rank. This performance was far better than for any other grouping of nations. Of the remaining nations, Horvat found that countries with a long welfare or social democratic tradition did better in the welfare comparison than did other developed capitalist countries where such a tradition was largely absent. However the difference between the "etatist" nations and the social democratic countries was greater than the difference between the latter and the remaining group of non-social democratic capitalist nations.

One problem with the Horvat study, however, which he himself concedes, is that the welfare rankings of the high income countries are biased downward and the welfare status of the poor countries is biased upwards. This is because at the upper end of the income scale the social welfare rank cannot be higher than the economic ranking; conversely at the lower end the social welfare ranking can hardly be lower than the income level. In fact it appears that this bias is quite important. The top thirteen countries in terms of income all rank relatively low in terms of the relationship between income and basic

* Horvat excludes Yugoslavia from the socialist bloc countries, but in the data collected below I include this country in the bloc. On the other hand he includes North Korea which I exclude on the grounds that data available for that country are too scarce to warrant its inclusion. All of the data employed by Horvat are taken from World Bank and United Nations sources.

welfare. At the same time eleven of the fourteen poorest nations possess social welfare levels higher than their economic development rank.

It is important therefore to try to correct for this bias and to determine whether it influenced Horvat's conclusion with respect to the welfare consequences of socialism. This is especially of interest since the nonwelfare state capitalist countries, the ones whose welfare rank were low compared to their incomes, were disproportionately included in the grouping of rich nations. Such nations were the United States, Canada, France, Germany (FR), Belgium and the Netherlands. The possibility arises, therefore, that Horvat's findings are spurious, the product of the bias mentioned above.

In order to check on the significance of this source of error the following proeedure was followed. Only countries ranked between 15 and 45 by income of the original sixty countries considered by Horvat were retained for examination, eliminating both the richest and poorest countries. By doing this we were able to eliminate the bias in Horvat's method as well as substantially compress the range of income differences present in the groupings of countries. At the same time all ten of the socialist bloc countries for whom adequate data are available were retained for consideration, thus facilitating the comparison of countries by their social organization.

The results of this retabulation are found in Table 3.1. They are clear and unambiguous. The elimination of the bias did not alter Horvat's conclusion. The "etatist" nations registered a basic welfare ranking below their per capita income level in only one of ten cases. Conversely the capitalist countries saw a basic welfare ranking below the income ranking in nine of twenty cases. The mean difference between income and basic welfare ranking for the socialist bloc was +5.1, meaning that on the average these countries ranked five places better in the welfare listing than on the income list. At the same time the capitalist countries mean difference came to –0.6. There thus seems little reason to quarrel with Horvat's original conclusion concerning the superiority of the socialist countries performance with respect to basic welfare. This conclusion takes on added force in light of the fact that this favorable welfare performance came at apparently no cost in terms of growth. Elsewhere in

Table 3.1

CAPITALIST AND SOCIALIST COUNTRIES BY RANKING OF PER CAPITA INCOME AND BASIC WELFARE

	1 1968 Per Capita Income	2 Basic Welfare	3 1–2		4 1968 Per Capita Income	5 Basic Welfare	6 4–5
Israel	16	11.3	+4.7	Germany (DR)	15	15.0	0.0
Puerto Rico	17	19.6	−2.6	Czechoslovakia	19	15.3	+3.7
Austria	18	19.0	−1.0	USSR	22	10.0	+11.4
Italy	20	14.3	+5.7	Hungary	23	24.3	−1.3
Japan	21	9.6	+11.4	Poland	26	22.3	+3.7
Ireland	24	21.3	+2.7	Romania	28	28.0	0.0
Venezuela	25	35.0	−10.0	Bulgaria	29	14.6	+14.4
Argentina	27	23.6	+3.4	Yugoslavia	33	28.0	+5.0
Greece	30	25.6	+4.4	Albania	40	30.3	+9.7
Spain	31	29.0	+2.0	Cuba	43	38.6	+4.4
Hong Kong	32	32.6	−0.6				
South Africa	34	46.0	−12.0				
Uruguay	36	30.6	+5.4				
Mexico	37	42.6	−5.6				
Chile	38	37.6	+0.4				
Portugal	39	34.3	+4.7				
Peru	41	38.0	+3.0				
Saudi Arabia	42	58.6	−16.6				
Malaysia	44	48.6	−4.6				
Guatamala	45	51.3	−6.3				

Revised and calculated from the source: Branco Horvat, "Welfare of the Common Man in Various Countries," Statistical Appendix I.

his article Horvat presents data which show that between 1960 and 1971 the socialist countries grew more rapidly than did comparable capitalist countries. (See Table 3.2.)

The experience of the socialist countries thus illustrates that growth and equity need not be seen as inevitably antagonistic. Whatever else may be said about the socialist bloc, it is clear

Table 3.2

AVERAGE ANNUAL RATE OF GROWTH OF REAL GNP PER CAPITA OF SOCIALIST AND CAPITALIST COUNTRIES BY INCOME LEVEL

Income Range (US dollars)	Socialist	Capitalist
200– 260	5.1	2.3
270– 560	5.8	2.7
650– 820	7.5	4.7
880–1230	5.4	5.0
1240–1620	4.2	4.7

Revised and calculated from the source: Branco Horvat, "Welfare of the Common Man in Various Countries," Statistical Appendix II.

that its countries have been able to achieve both high levels of economic growth and, at least, as compared to the experience of the capitalist countries, the provision of basic welfare needs. At once, therefore, this experience confirms the validity of the thesis presented by the "new economics of the less developed countries" that welfare considerations need not be sacrificed in order to achieve growth, but at the same time raises the question of whether this reconciliation can be achieved within a capitalist institutional framework.

It is possible at least to sketch a theory to account for the more favorable experience of the socialist countries compared to the capitalist countries in satisfying basic needs. The latter, it can be argued, are handicapped in two ways in trying to replicate the welfare pattern of the socialist bloc. On one hand the income distribution in capitalist societies critically depends upon the pattern of wealth ownership. Typically the property income which results from the latter is even more highly concentrated than the pattern which results from wages and salaries. Thus inequality is built into the very structure of a society in which the means of production are privately owned. To the extent that this is the case, of course, a concentrated pattern of income is extremely difficult to overcome. In this connection Ranis writes that "even if fiscal redistribution after the fact were politically and administratively feasible, it would have to assume completely unrealistic proportions to make a difference."[12]

The second problem concerns the role of the state. The provision of basic needs such as medical care, housing and education depends upon public allocations, particularly in underdeveloped countries. In both socialist and capitalist countries alike this requires the providing of social resources to the public sector. This is accomplished easily enough in the socialist context through the combining of price and tax policy. Revenues shifted to the state in such a situation may negatively affect demand, but with regard to resources available for investment, few consequences are likely. A shift of resources from the population generally to the public sector in order to finance welfare expenditures does not represent a reallocation away from would-be investors.

The converse is true in the context of capitalist under-development. In such a setting the presumption is that a large fraction of the population is too poor to be a fruitful source of tax revenues. The financing of public sector-provided basic needs must therefore come from the relatively affluent. But these are the potential savers and investors in the community. It is recognition of this conflict which is the source of the belief that growth and equity are in conflict under capitalism. For where the public sector expands it does so at the expense of savings and therefore limits investment. As a result growth can be retarded. This is all the more the case where dependency on external private investment prevails. In such a case an increase in the tax burden may deprive the host country of a firm's investment potential completely.

In theory, therefore, it is not difficult to discern why the socialist countries have done better with respect to the providing of basic needs than the capitalist underdeveloped countries. The contrasting structures of the two kinds of societies means that with respect to attaining a high degree of equality and the provision of public sector services the socialist mode of production has distinct structural advantages.

This then is the problem which confronts the advocates of the "new economics of the less developed countries." By and large they do not advocate a socialist mode of production, but yet at the same time they are alive to the human value implications of development without equity. Furthermore, they are aware that the failure to provide medical, educational and housing facilities in the context of economic development raises the question of political stability as well. The problem which may emerge is that the growth which is achieved will result in a rise in the aspirations of the people of a country, a rise which if left unresolved, may result in tensions and conflicts. It is in this way therefore that the issue of human values and aspirations has intruded itself in the area of economic development. Growth in the forces of production in and of itself does not satisfy human goals, but the degree to which the latter is accomplished helps to determine the viability of a social system. In short, the question posed by Marx in the 1850s – whether an expansion in the forces of production will emancipate or materially mend the condition of the masses of the people – remains alive today, and, as we shall see, was precisely the issues faced in the Caribbean in the 1970s.

NOTES

1. Marx and Engels, *Manifesto of the Communist Party*, as reprinted in Robert Freedman, ed., *Marx on Economics* (New York: Harcourt, Brace & Co., 1961), pp. 17, 26.
2. David Morawetz, *Twenty-Five Years of Economic Development 1950 to 1975* (Baltimore and London: The Johns Hopkins University Press, 1977), pp. 54–57.
3. Morawetz, *Twenty-Five Years of Economic Development*, p. 58.
4. Irma Adelman and Cynthia Taft Morris, "Growth and Impoverishment in the Middle of the Nineteenth Century," *World Development* 6, 3:246–247.
5. Nake M. Kamrany and John E. Elliott, "The North-South Dialogue," in Nake M. Kamrany, *The New Economics of the Less Developed Countries* (Boulder, Colorado: Westview Press, 1978), p. 1.
6. Benjamin Higgins, "Economic Development and Cultural Change: Seamless Web or Patchwork Quilt?" in Manning Nash, ed., *Essays on* Economic Development and Cultural Change in Honor of Bert F. Roselitz, *Economic Development and Cultural Change* 25, supplement 1977, p. 100.
7. Gustav Ranis, "Development Theory at Three Quarters Century," in Manning Nash, ed., *Essays on Economic Development and Cultural Change*, pp. 256–257.
8. Morawetz, *Twenty-Five Years of Economic Development*, p. 7.

9. Karl Marx, "The Future Results of British Rule in India," in Shlomo Avineri, ed., *Karl Marx Colonialism and Modernization* (Garden City, Doubleday Press & Co., 1968), p. 129.
10. Branko Horvat, "Welfare of the Common Man in Various Countries," *World Development* 2, 7(July 1974):31.
11. Horvat, "Welfare of the Common Man," p. 32.
12. Ranis, "Development Theory at Three Quarters Century," p. 257.

Chapter 4

The Plantation Mode of Production and Development

The view adopted here is that the capability and motivation to introduce new methods of production are influenced by the class structure of society. The mere presence of a group of profit-seekers is not sufficient to ensure extensive technological advance. Whether profit-seekers engage in technological innovation or not depends upon the extent to which both the ability and incentive to do so is sufficiently present. Thus, historical data which show that one or more sets of class relations are promotive of both the capability and the desire to innovate will be interpreted as evidence that development was encouraged under such a regime. Where, however, a pattern of class relations is shown to be negatively associated with either the demand or the supply of new technology it will be considered to form an inhospitable environment for economic development.

An alternative view – that the spread of economic development was limited because of the difficulty of implementing the new methods of production – can safely be ruled out at least for the nineteenth century, the period which concerns us in this chapter. As Arthur Lewis notes, the new techniques of production of the early industrial revolution "... were ingenious, but simple to apply."[1] Possible constraints to the adoption of the new methods such as large capital requirements or the need to capture economies of scale were virtually absent. The explanation of the failure to employ such new methods thus resides in one or more aspects of the societies which failed to do so, rather than because these new methods of production may have been particularly difficult to master, expensive or required large market outlets.

The presence of a growth-inhibiting social structure has dominated the history of the Caribbean. This mode of production – a plantation economy – was constructed in those parts of the region where European expansion took the form of establishing large scale farms in order to supply metropolitan markets with tropical or semitropical staples. The thesis presented here is that the functioning of the plantation mode of production differed from capitalism and that, unlike a capitalist mode of production, militated against economic development.

In a plantation mode of production four attributes are present. First, large scale export-oriented agriculture dominates the society. Second, the labor force requirements of that agricultural sector are greater than can be supplied through the functioning of a domestic labor market. Third, as a result, a nonmarket mechanism of mobilizing and allocating labor is present and this mechanism is dominant in defining the class relations of the society. Finally, a specific culture both emerges from and reinforces the class relations which are articulated in this way.

Defined in this way Plantation America extended from "about midway up the coast of Brazil into the Guianas, along the Caribbean coast, throughout the Caribbean itself and into the United States."[2] Here a slave-based agriculture was established dating from the 17th century. Even after emancipation in the 19th century, however, nowhere in this region did market mechanisms become dominant in determining where labor worked, in what numbers and at what levels of reward. Labor, in short, after emancipation, as before, continued to be made available to plantations in larger numbers and at lower costs than would have been present if a free market had been fully operative. The central issue to be analyzed in this chapter is why these societies failed to achieve modern economic development. For, as noted by Eugene D. Genovese and Elizabeth Fox-Genovese, "no slaveholdings country or region crossed the threshold to industrialization and none adjusted to emancipation so as to launch a new cycle of growth that passed into structural development."[3]

The societies of Plantation America were all new societies in the sense that when they were settled by Europeans an indigenous culture and society was either nonexistent or was soon to be decimated. The societies which emerged, therefore, were societies unencumbered by persisting aspects of a previous social structure. What did influence the organization of such societies were the concerns and interests of the European settlers, as influenced by the requirements of climate, technology, and difficulties in gaining access to a suitable labor force.

The central problem for such societies was the question of labor scarcity. There was ample opportunity to produce and market an export staple. But the technology available to do so required large numbers of workers, many times more than were locally available. The use of a domestic labor market to satisfy the needs of the planters was, therefore, out of the question. So too was participation in an international labor market since immigration would have required wage rates whose high level would have severely constrained output. To produce in large volume, as the planters desired to do, meant finding a means whereby labor would be made available for production but at substantially lower costs than would prevail if a labor market were functioning.

The by-passing of the labor market meant that these societies were organized in a way different than a capitalist economy is structured. For as Maurice Dobb has noted, under capitalism propertyless workers provide their labor "... not by virtue of legal compulsion but on the basis of a wage contract" voluntarily entered into.[4] Clearly, therefore, in these societies a salient feature of capitalism was absent. This absence, however, had profound implications. For, as we shall argue, the use of force in mobilizing and allocating labor played a causal role in the fact that none of these plantation dominated societies experienced modern economic development.

The classic nonmarket mechanism employed in this regard was slavery. It was the use of violence implicit in the institution of chattel slavery which provided labor to the plantations. Its purpose was to do so at costs lower than would have prevailed in a setting in which labor could choose whether to supply itself or not. This, of course, is not to argue that there were no costs involved in gaining access to and mobilizing a plantation labor force. During the era of the slave trade the costs associated with the search for and transportation of slaves on the plantations necessitated large outlays by the planters. But the price of slaves was established in a market different from a labor market. Workers in the latter were voluntary participants while, by definition, the slaves were not free agents. As a result of that difference, in the Southern United States for example Fogel and Engerman estimate that "... the application of force made it possible to obtain labor from slaves at less than half the price that would have had to have been offered in the absence of force."[5]

Still a problem remained for the planters. Having purchased slaves, they had gained access to a potential source of work. But it yet remained for the planters to exact that work from the slaves. The planters had purchased "labor" but not yet "labor power." For that to be accomplished interaction with the slaves themselves was necessary.

In principle obtaining a slave's agreement to work could have been accomplished in two possible ways. In the first case direct force and coercion could have been employed. In the last extreme this could have meant threatening the slaves with death unless work was forthcoming. At the opposite end of the spectrum planters could have offered concessions – either material or otherwise – in an exchange for the labor of the plantation workers. In practice, no doubt, various combinations of these extremes were employed. It is important to note, however, that even where concessions were employed it was violence and force upon which the system rested. "Property rights in man" could only be attained through coercion, even where relations between master and slave were tempered by a degree of mutual accommodation.

Where two circumstances were present planters were unlikely to grant significant concessions. One was a context in which ecological circumstances resulted in high levels of mortality.[6] Especially in tropical climates, as opposed to the semitropical conditions of the United States South, disease control was beyond either the scientific capacity or financial interests of the planter class. In such circumstances the cost to the planter of the use of force was less than it would have been if mortality were under better control. The death of a slave did not mean as much foregone production as it would have in healthier circumstances since the probabilities of death were high in any case. Similarly, where absentee-ownership was prevalent, benevolent paternalism did not emerge as a potent instrument. To the extent that plantation authority was vested in an overseer rather than in the hands of a participating planter, the moral authority of the latter was absent in the relations between slave and plantation manager. The overseer in these circumstances could not confidently call on noncoercive techniques to accomplish the plantations' ends.

The situation was different in the United States South. In his book, *Roll, Jordan, Roll* Eugene D. Genovese writes:

> The slaveholders of the South, unlike those of the Caribbean, increasingly resided on their plantations and by the end of the eighteenth century had become an entrenched regional ruling class. The paternalism encouraged by the close living of masters and slaves was enormously reinforced by the closing of the African slave trade which compelled masters to pay greater attention to the reproduction of their labor force.

In this context brute force was augmented with a complex cultural bond between chattel and master. As Genovese puts it:

> Paternalism defined the involuntary labor of the slaves as a legitimate return to their masters for production and direction. But, the masters' need to see their slaves as acquiescent human beings constituted a moral victory for the slaves themselves. Paternalism's insistence upon mutual obligations – duties, responsibilities and ultimately even rights – implicitly recognized the slaves' humanity.[7]

The existence of a paternalistic culture in the United States South but not elsewhere in the Caribbean did not mean, however, that different modes of production existed in these two areas of Plantation America. Even in the case of the United States the use of force was never very far in the background. The means by which planter domination was achieved varied according to circumstances. But the presence of paternalism did mean that in the United States South force was more latent than in other parts of the plantation America.

Slave emancipation occurred in the British Caribbean in the 1830s, in the United States in the 1860s, and in Brazil as late as the 1880s. Whenever it occurred, however, the slave labor force attempted in droves to vacate the plantations, eagerly seeking out alternative employment opportunities. In the process, everywhere the estates themselves confronted the threat of financial crisis and potential ruin. For while the product market for most plantation commodities remained firm, the plantations' depleted manpower reserves severely limited their ability to produce.

Slave emancipation, then, marked a major choice point in the evolution of plantation economies. In principle, three resolutions were possible to the crisis attendant upon emancipation. The first was what the planters feared most. Unable to reorganize production in the aftermatch of the loss of their slave population, the estates would go under. Land would increasingly be made available for sale. The final result of this process would be the developing of a peasantry, cultivating former plantation land. A second possible outcome could have been the estates remaining intact but with production reorganized using new and advanced technology. In this way the ownership structure of the economy might remain similar as before. However with the drastically reduced supply of labor available for plantation work, the new technology would result in a corresponding reduction in the demand for labor. It is likely, though not certain, that under these circumstances the need for coercion too might have declined. If so, then plantation agriculture would have been converted to free-labor capitalist agriculture and the plantation economy would have come to an end. The last possibility was the reestablishment of the plantation economy on some other basis than slavery. With slavery abolished, this necessitated finding some alternative mechanism whereby labor would be made available to the estates at wages lower than they would have been if workers were free to choose among various occupations. Involved here was the need for the presence of some mechanism to prevent alternative employment opportunities from being made available to potential plantation workers.

In both the British Caribbean and the American South, the financial crisis which confronted the plantations in the aftermath of emancipation was real and severe. And this was so in the former case despite the fact that the British government compensated the planters for the loss of their "property." For while such compensation tended to offset the financial loss attendant upon emancipation, it did not assure a continued supply of workers to the plantations. It was this labor supply problem which held the key to the future viability of the estates.

If freedom meant that the former slave population was to be permitted to work at nonplantation occupations, then the logic of emancipation implied the demise of the plantation. This was so because under free market circumstances few former slaves would choose to work on the estates at wage rates profitable to the planters. But this undermining of the plantation economy was not the immediate result of emancipation. The continued viability of plantation agriculture even after emancipation was based on the fact that the newly freed slaves had little influence on governmental policymaking. As a result the policies required to give real content to freedom were not carried out. Indeed in some cases like that of Trinidad and Guyana just the opposite was the case; policies were followed with the intention of rehabilitating the plantations. Elsewhere official neglect of the former slaves ensured their continued subordination, and, in the aftermath of emancipation, nonplantation employment for the ex-slaves was largely foreclosed. As a result plantation agriculture drew new life.

Land policy was the key to the problem of alternative employment opportunities. For if land had been made available to the former slaves, its availability would have represented precisely the alternative which would have doomed the plantations. As a result, throughout the region planters struggled to ensure that land was not made accessible to the former slaves. To the extent that they were successful in this blocking effort, the planters succeeded in insulating themselves from the need to compete for a labor force.

The means by which land acquisition were stymied varied. In some of the smaller islands of the West Indies the planters already owned all of the cultivatable land. Hence it was not difficult to prevent the emergence of an independent peasantry. As Hugh Tinker puts it with regard to Barbados, it was possible to bond most of the former slaves to the plantations because "though people might now be free – the land remained in bondage."[8] Land simply was not sold to former slaves. Nonplantation work could be obtained, therefore, only by leaving the island, an act impossible for virtually all of the former slave population. In such circumstances formal slave emancipation was largely drained of its economic meaning because of the absence of choice with regard to employment and plantation agriculture proceeded with little disruption.

In the United States South the possibility was somewhat greater that the ex-slaves would be able to escape the confines of the plantation. The former slaves themselves believed that with emancipation they would be granted agricultural land, thereby freeing them from the necessity of plantation work. No such program of land reform ever became a reality. The radicals in Congress who advocated such a program could never pass the necessary legislation. Indeed just the opposite appears to have occurred on an informal basis within the South. Great social pressures were mounted against those white landowners who even considered selling plantation land to former slaves. This "imperfection" in the market for land meant that the former slaves were deprived of even that land which they might expect to gain access to through the operation of a competitive market in which they willingly were allowed to bid a price. When finally a black landowning class did emerge in the South, it developed under circumstances distinctly nonthreatening to the planters in areas outside of the plantation hegemony. Thus, the "black belt" was the region most dominated by plantation cultivation, but in 1910, for example, was the part of the South least characterized by black landownership.[9] Within the plantation sphere black landownership was still severely limited.

The denial of land in the South was probably the most important but certainly not the only means by which the ex-slave population in the United States was constrained to plantation work. Evidence indicates that racist employer attitudes in manufacturing in the North denied that avenue of escape to the plantation workers. Instead of recruiting black labor from the South, industrialists hired immigrants arriving from Europe. The denial to blacks of northern employment opportunities was further reinforced by southern state and local legislation. Anti-enticement and recruiting legislation served to raise the cost of such recruiting. Even if a northern employer had wished to hire black labor, the costs of doing so were raised by these legislative barriers, thus tending to reduce the outflow from the South of such labor.[10]

The problem of land policy was even more critical for the planters in Caribbean areas of "open resources." In regions where the person/land ratio was low, ex-slaves not only desired to leave the plantations, but they had the opportunity to do so as well. In Guyana, for example, squatting on Crown Lands occurred in significant numbers in the aftermath of emancipation. The cultivation of this land represented a real alternative to plantation labor, and threatened to produce a severe disruption of estate cultivation.

To preserve plantation agriculture, therefore, it was essential that this alternative be minimized. And this was exactly what the colonial government attempted to do in Guyana. Its effort was to make the terms of purchase of land as arduous as possible in order to discourage the emergence of a peasant sector which would be competitive with the plantation sector. It did so not so much by fixing a high price per acre of land sold, but rather by establishing a 100-acre lot size as the minimum which could be purchased. In doing so it put the cost of land beyond all potential purchasers except existing plantation owners. In this way the emergence of a peasant sector was aborted and in the process the possibility of competition for labor between the plantation and peasant sector foreclosed.[11]

In Guyana and Trinidad and to a more limited extent elsewhere in the British Caribbean, the colonial governments turned to the outside to find a new labor force for the plantations. The history of indentured immigration, largely from India, to the Caribbean is well-known, and need not be repeated here. It is sufficient to note, however, that through virtually all of the nineteenth century land policy was such that it continued to be very difficult for estate laborers – of Indian or African descent – to gain access to arable acreage. Though the terms of indenture changed somewhat over time, a continual flow of workers bound to plantations for between five and ten years continued in the region until World War I. With immigration augmenting the supply of plantation labor and land policy constraining its depletion, estate cultivation was protected and encouraged.

The post-emancipation period throughout Plantation America, then, demonstrated that plantation agriculture did not depend upon slavery. Other mechanisms could be activated to perpetuate the result that slavery had successfully achieved. What plantation agriculture required was an abundant supply of cheap labor. Slavery had provided this to the estates; but so too could a policy of land denial to the ex-slaves, especially when such a policy was backed up by racial discrimination, sharecropping or indentured immigration. By taking advantage of these mechanisms, plantation agriculture could be retained as a profitable way to carry out agricultural production.

No plantation economy ever achieved modern economic development. One way to see why this was so is to think of the introduction of new technology as being subject to two principal considerations. The first is the incentives planters possess to adopt new technology. With planters assumed to be motivated by the search for profit, the issue is the extent to which profits are sought through the introduction of new methods of production or new crops. The second consideration relates to the capacity to introduce new technology. Here the issue addresses the question of the availability of a stock of relevant knowledge and information. Even a planter motivated to achieve technological progress might be unable to do so if, for the crops which are under cultivation or which are being considered for cultivation, new techniques of production are unavailable. The hypothesis presented here is that the failure of economic development in plantation economies flows from the fact that such a society is relatively disadvantaged with respect both to the incentive and capability of adopting new technology.

The extent to which planters were motivated to seek out new methods of production was limited in two ways. Assuming that labor was rendered relatively inexpensive because of the by-passing of the labor market, a profit-maximizing planter would tend to use relatively more labor and relatively less tools and equipment than would be the case if labor's price were closer to its free market equilibrium. The typical plantation production function thus was labor intensive. Such a pattern of production, however, militates against technological advance since new technology is often embodied in new capital equipment and tools. The effect, therefore, of circumventing the labor market was to reduce the amount of capital used in production. In doing so capital as a carrier of new technology too was minimized, tending to depress the rate of productivity advance. It was precisely because the planters were cost minimizers that they deemphasized the use of capital in production. But as a result so the plantation society's rate of technological advancement suffered compared to market economies where labor may have been relatively more expensive.

In addition to the fact that the factor proportions employed by planters tended to reduce the extent of technological change, there is a second reason to believe that the search for new techniques was limited in plantation economies. In reviewing historical episodes the outcomes of which were advances in production techniques, Nathan Rosenberg identified three "focusing devices" – experiences which tended to intensify the search for new methods of production.[12] The three focusing devices cited by Rosenberg were technical imbalances in the production process, the threat of labor shortages and disruptions in the supply of essential materials. Both the first and third of these mechanisms are more appropriate to manufacturing than agriculture. It is therefore not remarkable that they were not present in plantation economies, for in agriculture the sequencing of the stages of production occurs over a longer time span than in manufacturing. Problems of coordination are less acute than in manufacturing. Similarly the availability of raw materials is a less serious problem in agriculture than in manufacturing because of the greater self-reliance in agriculture's production process. The problem of the labor supply, on the other hand, is not one which agriculture escapes. It is in this regard that the functioning of the plantation economy tended to reduce the incentive to adopt new technology.

Rosenberg cites England during the industrial revolution as an illustration of a case where the reluctance of labor to accept factory discipline provided an incentive to adopt labor-saving technology. According to him the risk of withdrawal of labor and the development of labor scarcities focused the attention of decision-makers on this potential threat to profits. As a result this threat acted as a focusing device and spurred industrialists to change methods of production.

The plantation economy was an unlikely place to find this kind of mechanism. For the very foundation of the plantation economy – the denial of freedom to the labor force – was structured exactly to avoid these kinds of production disruptions. To the extent that the repressive institutions of the plantation economy – preeminently the institution of slavery – were successfully functioning and allowing for the viability of plantation agriculture at all, they were also acting to minimize the appearance of such a focusing device.

We thus can identify two reasons to believe that under the regime of the plantation economy, the incentive to search out and adopt new technologies was less than it would have been under a free labor regime. The first stemmed from the fact that under plantation circumstances labor was cheaper to the planter than it otherwise would have been. The second was the consequence of the fact that unfree labor was much less likely to be disruptive to production than free workers.

But not only was the search for productivity improvement constrained in the plantation economy. Even if there had been an intense desire for such advances, problems with respect to the availability of such new techniques would have created substantial difficulties. Significantly, however, at least in part these problems of the "supply" of new technology too can be traced to the structure of the plantation economy.

In the first place many of the technical problems associated with tropical or semitropical agriculture were difficult. For example, in the harvesting of cotton the developing of a mechanical picker was particularly a problem because the bolls on the cotton ripen unevenly. A mechanical picker was therefore required to leave intact and uninjured some bolls, while harvesting others. Similarly in sugar the stalk had to be harvested with little or no damage, often in terrain which constrained the weight of the harvester. Furthermore the cut in the stalk was required to be clean so as to minimize the loss of the stalk's sucrose content.[13]

While these difficulties presented special challenges, the evidence indicates that they were not decisive in limiting the availability of new techniques; what appears to be even more important than technical difficulties was the only limited extent to which there was a search for such new techniques. Here again we are returned to the consequences of the structure of the plantation economy. To the extent that the population of such a society was enslaved or bound, it was not possessed with the skills, opportunities, or incentives to engage in such a search. Thus, without even taking into account the question of whether the culture of the planter class militated against scientific advance, the disadvantage of the plantation economy compared to a freer economy with respect to the ability and opportunity to search for and introduce new methods of production is obvious. The very mechanisms by which plantations were rendered commercially viable involved decreasing the proportion of the population motivated and even physically able to undertake the kind of experimentation and trial and error processes necessary to advance production methods. As a result, the admittedly difficult technical problems of harvesting plantation crops could not have been the object of the kind of attention which may well have existed in nonplantation settings.

If ever, however, there had been a focusing device, an increase in the demand for technological change, emancipation must have been it. No more profound disruption in a labor supply system could be imagined than the ending of slavery. The entire institutionalized pattern upon which plantation agriculture rested had been dismantled. To compensate for the loss of their labor force, planters must have confronted a greatly increased incentive to increase the estate's level of labor productivity. Yet so far as the literature records, no prolonged intensified search for new labor saving methods of production occurred in this period. Indeed the fact that the subject is infrequently recorded in the discussion of the immediate aftermath of slavery may represent the most profound evidence that this presumed increased incentive to adopt new methods of production was not acted upon by the former slave owners.

The heritage of the slave period weighs heavily in accounting for the failure of technological change with emancipation. First, the stock of knowledge necessary to introduce new techniques clearly was inadequate in this period to allow for the rapid introduction of new techniques. Such information might either be formally scientific in the sense that it emerged from controlled experimentation or else it might be "folk" knowledge gleaned from everyday trial and error efforts. In either case, however, the knowledge available and relevant to plantation staples was limited. This, of course, was the heritage of slavery in which decision-makers faced only a severely constrained incentive to search for such information.

The second consequence of the slave period relevant to this

issue relates specifically to the capacities of the planters. These were men who were now called upon to adopt an entirely new approach to production. In the past, labor, through the institution of slavery, always had been the key to the planter's ability to produce profitability. Now under the threat of labor scarcity, one possible response would be to turn increasingly to science and technology as an answer to their production and profitability problems. To do so, however, was at best difficult and for some planters impossible. Given a long enough period of labor scarcity, some planters, no doubt, would have accomplished this transition. But habits of mind and patterns of life meant that it was a difficult change for all. Furthermore, in many cases, emancipation meant at least short-term financial distress, undermining the planters ability to innovate, even if they had wanted to do so. As a result for most, at least during the immediate aftermath of slavery, there was little search for new production methods. Rather the search was for new methods of slavery: to discover new ways by which the traditional pattern of production could be retained.

There was one important exception to this pattern, but this exception tends, in fact, to support the hypothesis presented here. According to Richard Lobdell "large foreign-based, vertically integrated companies" became increasingly important in the region during the last two-thirds of the nineteenth century. These new firms, he argues, were technological innovators to a greater extent than already resident companies and plantations. Lobdell specifically argues that the "new enterprises were no longer bound by the tradition, nostalgia and status consideration which had proved so important to earlier planters."[14] In making this comparison of course, Lobdell at least indirectly provides evidence concerning the cultural incapacity of the older plantation owners to carry through the innovations which the newer group demonstrated to be technically feasible.

Overall then, as great as the incentive to adopt new technology may have been, the unavailability of such new techniques, and the limited capacities of the producers to search out such new techniques, militated against the immediate introduction of labor saving production methods. At least in the short-run, the problems related to the supply of new technology overwhelmed the impact of the demand for such innovations. Both, – the incentive to adopt new technology and the stock of knowledge necessary for such an adoption to occur – were constrained in a plantation economy. The planters normally did not face a strong incentive to adopt such techniques, and even when they did it is likely that such new technology would have been available only to a limited extent. Both the limited demand for and the supply of new technology had their roots in the structure of the plantation economy. In this way, therefore, the structure of the plantation economy acted to constrain the emergence of the new technology.

The plantation economy was a growth-inhibiting mode of production. Its productive relations – the coerced status of its labor force – acted as a fetter on the development of its forces of production. In this sense the plantation economy takes a place among those modes of production which retarded development. Created as a result of the expansion of European capitalism, precisely the mechanisms required to satisfy the demand of world markets for tropical and semitropical staples meant that the plantation economy was not fully capitalist. It further meant that this mode of production constrained its own technological advance. It was, thus, with the plantation economy in place, that the Caribbean became an underdeveloped region.

NOTES

1. W. Arthur Lewis, "The Diffusion of Development" in Thomas Wilson and Andrew S. Skinner, eds., *The Market and the State, Essays in Honour of Adam Smith* (Oxford: Clarendon Press, 1976), pp. 136–137.
2. Charles Wagley, "Plantation America: A Culture Sphere," in Vera Rubin, ed., *Caribbean Studies: A Symposium* (Seattle: University of Washington Press, 1960), p. 5.
3. Eugene D. Genovese and Elizabeth Fox-Genovese, "The Slave Economies in Political Perspective," *The Journal of American History* 66, 1 (June 1979):11.
4. Maurice Dobb, *Studies in the Development of Capitalism* (New York: International Publishers, 1947), p. 9.
5. Robert William Fogel and Stanley L. Engerman, *Time on the Cross: The Economics of American Negro Slavery* (Boston: Little, Brown & Company, 1974), I, p. 238.
6. B. W. Higman, *Slave Population and Economy in Jamaica 1807–1834* (Cambridge: Cambridge University Press, 1976), pp. 99–138.

7. Eugene D. Genovese, *Roll, Jordan, Roll: The World the Slaves Made* (New York: Pantheon, 1975), p. 5.
8. Hugh Tinker, *A New System of Slavery: The Export of Indian Labour Overseas 1830–1920* (London: Oxford University Press, 1974), p. 2.
9. Jay R. Mandle, *The Roots of Black Poverty: The Southern Plantation Economy after the Civil War* (Durham: Duke University Press, 1978), p. 43.
10. Mandle, *The Roots of Black Poverty*, Chapter 2.
11. For more on this, see Jay R. Mandle, *The Plantation Economy: Population and Economic Changes in Guyana 1838–1960* (Philadelphia: Temple University Press, 1973), Chapter 3.
12. Nathan Rosenberg, "The Direction of Technological Change: Inducement Mechanism and Focusing Devices," *Economic Development and Cultural Change*, Vol. 18, October 1969.
13. See Andrew M. Kamark, *The Tropics and Economic Development: A Provocative Inquiry into the Poverty of Nations* (Baltimore: The Johns Hopkins University Press, 1976) for a discussion of the special problem of tropical agriculture.
14. Richard A. Lobdell, "Patterns of Investment and Sources of Credit in the British West Indian Sugar Industry, 1838–96," *The Journal of Caribbean History*, Volume 4, May 1972, p. 53.

Chapter 5

Dependent Development in the Caribbean

As we saw in chapter 1 the evidence suggests that after about 1950 economic growth increasingly was experienced in the relatively poor countries of the world. Though Bairoch's data may exaggerate the rate of this expansion, there seems little reason to doubt the general pattern which emerges from his studies. The years after 1950 represent the period in which the onset of economic development was widely experienced.

The experience of the Caribbean generally conforms to the timing of the onset of growth sketched here. As we saw in chapter 4, the functioning of the plantation economy generally inhibited economic development. But after World War II the institutions which prevented economic expansion were largely dismantled and this region joined with other poor countries in its first period of sustained growth.

The plantation economy of the Caribbean was not seriously challenged until the 1930s. Then, under mounting pressure from the international depression, the West Indian population reached a point of explosion. During 1937 and 1938 a succession of riots and insurrections swept the English speaking Caribbean in an unorganized but profound rebellion. Gordon K. Lewis writes of these uprisings as

> the revolt of West Indian peasants and workers against a society in which, despite formal emancipation, they were still regarded merely as suppliers of cheap labor to sugar kings and oil barons in search of quick profits. Slavery had been abolished; but the economic foundation of slavery, especially in the general picture of land ownership had remained basically untouched.[1]

In the first instance the British responded to these outbreaks by appointing an investigating commission – the West India Royal Commission – known as the Moyne Commission. The Commission understood that the fundamental problem in the region was the failure of economic development. It wrote that what was required was "a substantial and steady increase in the volume of economic activity." However it was notably cautious in recommending means to achieve such an economic advance. It did not, for example, believe that industrial development was possible in the region. Though the Commission did recommend encouraging the development of a peasantry, it nonetheless believed that "the majority of the population must continue to depend for a long period, if not indefinitely on export agriculture." The Moyne Commission did not, in short, foresee the possibility of breaking out of the plantation economy.[2]

Despite this official conservatism, however, it was in these years that the Caribbean plantation economy was dismantled. The plantation mode of production required the provision of a docile and chap labor force. The region-wide insurrections of 1937–1938, however, were the first signal that the century-old post-emancipation mechanisms of control had finally worn thin. Soon to follow, in the 1940s, was the emergence of a nationalist politics, especially in the larger territories, and the development of mass-based trade union movements. Increasingly in these years plantation managers and owners confronted a labor force which, from their point of view, was unreliable and potentially disruptive, characteristics inconsistent with the dictates of plantation agriculture.

The classic response to these tendencies occurred in Guyana. There the sugar industry in the late 1940s undertook, for the first time, to expand output by raising levels of labor productivity. Always before in the past when growth was desired it was accomplished simply by increasing acreage and manpower used in the production. Under the new circumstances this approach was now considered excessively risky and intensive growth was essayed. This reaction was replicated throughout the region and was a response to a phenomenon which was also region-wide. The West Indian population no longer would accept its role as semi-slaves; as a result the old system of plantation agriculture was no longer viable.

The question which immediately arose, however, concerned the nature of the economy which would replace the plantation mode of production. It was the St. Lucian-born economist, W. Arthur Lewis, who supplied the answer in the late 1940s.

Lewis was the first Caribbean economist to appreciate both the possibility and necessity for industrialization in the region as an alternative to continued reliance on the export of agricultural staples.

In contrast to the prevailing orthodoxy of the period he argued that continued export agriculture specialization would doom the region to mounting unemployment and poverty. To avoid this he advocated a program by which manufacturing would absorb the growing labor force of the area. He showed that despite the region's small size an impressive array of industries were in fact commercially feasible.[3] To accomplish this end the Caribbean would have to become a welcoming society. It would achieve economic advance by attracting private foreign investment especially in export-oriented manufacturing industries. The technological stagnation of the plantation economy was to be replaced by the progressivity associated with foreign capital and production methods. Full integration into the world capitalist economy was envisioned.

The creation of new industries, Lewis argued, required foreign capital. It was necessary, he asserted, to "try to persuade existing suppliers, with established distribution channels in Latin America, to open factories in the islands to supply their trade." The argument that such investment come from expatriate sources was defended on three grounds: the region was thought not to be capable of generating the savings necessary for the "frightfully expensive" process of industrialization; regional businessmen tended to specialize in agriculture and commerce and were not sufficiently experienced in manufacturing; and gaining access to the required markets could more easily be achieved through already existing channels than by new firms attempting to break into already existing markets. Because of the need for foreign capital and capitalists, wrote Lewis, there was a need for "a period of wooing and fawning upon such people." Specifically, he argued that "what the West Indies would have to do is to try to get some English and United States manufacturers . . . to start factories in the West Indies in addition to or in place of their factories elsewhere. . . ."[4]

In the Lewis strategy the principal attraction of the region for a foreign firm was the prevailing low level of wages. For products in which labor costs were a significant fraction of total outlays in production, the region could offer the prospect of low costs and potential high profits to businesses. In order futher to make the region attractive to would-be investors, Lewis also recommended the creation of a region-wide Industrial Development Corporation and Industrial Development Bank. While loans would be offered through the latter institution, the former would promote the region to businesses abroad, and especially point to the fact that wages in the areas were only one-fifth of the level of the United States. In addition, it would offer to build and even operate suitable factories in order to demonstrate their economic feasibility.[5]

The general outlines of the Lewis strategy of "industrialization by invitation" became official policy in the region during the 1950s. All parts the anglophone Caribbean declared it their aim to industrialize and to that end established industrial development corporations as suggested by Lewis. Furthermore each colony offered tax and fiscal incentives in an effort to attract investment capital. The absence of economic integration during this period meant that the wooing of foreign investment did not occur on the kind of regional basis suggested by Lewis. Nonetheless, it is clear that Lewis' work was quite influential both in identifying the need for industrialization and in suggesting the means for achieving that end in the region.

There is, of course, plausibility to the development strategy outlined by Lewis. It is consistent with an ideology which envisions the spread of capitalist economic development from developed to the less developed regions as a process primarily motivated by market signals. The argument is that the presence of low wage rates means that anticipated rates of return on investment are higher than normal. Mobile investment capital, according to the theory, responds to the opportunity which these high rates of return make available and migrates to such an area. This, in turn, tends to increase the level of economic development, in the process narrowing the gap between rich and poor regions.

The world view which underlies this theory is one of harmony, balance and integration. It presumes the functioning of an equilibrium-generating social mechanism. When differences between regions or countries become marked, self-correcting forces are put to work, tending to eliminate those discontinuities. Thus the interests of one region are seen as complementary to those of another since advances in one will, with the passage of time, produce advances in the other area. In Lewis' version an active promotional role is envisioned for the state in achieving such an equilibrium. Even here, though, such a role presumes the existence of tendencies promoting convergence, and the role of policy is simply to encourage that process.

Market-oriented outward looking strategies of economic growth have been implemented in countries such as Korea, Ivory Coast, Kenya and Brazil. In these and other such nations expansion has occurred as they purposefully placed themselves and actively participated in world market structures. The growth which has been achieved attests to the fact that it is possible to avoid being overwhelmed by the backwash effects hypothesized by Gunnar Myrdal.[6] Instead of losing capital and skilled manpower to the metropolitan countries and suffering an adverse movement in their terms of trade, these countries have beenfitted from contact with the developed nations. Especially through the agency of international corporations they have been the net recipients of capital and technology. Similarly multinational corporations contributed to the diversification of their production structures. In this way they have protected countries against the risk of a deterioration in the relative prices of the goods they produced. Finally through international firms these countries have gained access to market outlets which otherwise might have been foreclosed to them.

The pattern described here has been characterized by several authorities as "dependent development." Thus Fernando Henrique Cardoso writes that the contemporary character of dependency "does not conflict with the economic development of dependent economies."[7] In arguing in this way, such authorities point to the changes which have occurred in recent years to the composition of foreign investment. Gone are the days when foreign investment in poor countries was confined to agriculture and the extraction of raw materials. Now throughout Latin America, Africa and Asia the pattern of investment by multinational corporations has shifted to manufacturing. Citing this shift Cardoso argues that

> The point is not only that multinational corporations are investing in the industrial sectors of dominated economies instead of traditional agricultural and mineral sectors. Beyond that even in "traditional" sectors of dependent economies, they are operating in technically and organizationally advanced modes, sometimes accepting local participation in these enterprises."[8]

As a result not only is output increasing in such nations, but as well the structural changes associated with economic development – changes in the composition of output and the industrial structure of the labor force – are also occurring. In this way, writes Cordoso, "there exists simultaneously a process of dependency and capitalist development."[9]

Peter Evans' study of contemporary Brazil stands as a case study which provides empirical support for Cardoso's views. Like Cardoso, Evans emphasizes the importance of an alliance between local and foreign capital and the state sector. Evans writes that with regard to Brazil "foreign capital . . . shares with local capital, both private and state-controlled, an interest in the further development of local industry."[10] By virtue of their access to capital and their organizational and technological capacity international corporations have played a critical role in the expansion of Brazil's economy in the last two decades.

To be sure the profit motivated interests of such firms and the developmental requirements of the economy not infrequently fail to coincide. Thus for example, multinational firms have preferred to maintain their research and development efforts in the metropolitan country. In an effort to protect their monopoly control over products and techniques they have preferred not to relocate such efforts in countries such as Brazil. Such a reluctance is, however, undesirable from the point of view of the poor country. Technological advance appropriate to local circumstances would be provided with a further impetus if research and development efforts were undertaken on-site. There thus arises a need "to redirect the global rationality of the multinational when it conflicts with the necessity of local accumulation."[11] This job of redirection falls to the second partner in the alliance, the government of the poor country.

In the first instance the role of the state is to ensure that multinational firms invest in the host country. To accomplish this goal, rules of the game which assure above normal profits to the enterprise must be constructed and these rules be respected. Within these rules, however, there is room for maneuver. Bargaining between the state and the multinational can occur in which the former attempts to bring the latter's behavior more in line with the development requirements of the country than would otherwise be the case.

In the bargaining which occurs the state's position is strengthened to the extent that the developing country possesses attributes promotive of the firm's profitability. Such resources are the existence of an extensive local market, a low wage labor force, or of course, a valuable natural resource. The presence of one or more of these provides the state with leverage and may enable it to coax developmental behavior from what otherwise might be a reluctant partner. In these circumstances too the state must as well possess the technical competence for it to be a credible bargaining adversary.

Compared to the multinational firms and the government, local capital in dependent development plays the role of third and junior partner. At least in Brazil however, as described by Evans, this role is still significant. On one hand it functions in sectors of the economy which are not of interest to the international corporations. On the other hand it plays what Evans calls an "integrative" function, facilitating the entrance of expatriates into dialogue with important local decision-makers.[12]

Though affirming the authenticity of dependent development, Evans is skeptical concerning its universality. He writes that "dependent development is not a phase that all peripheral countries will be able to reach. Only a few are chosen." He hypothesizes that smallness of size reduces the attractiveness of a country to a multinational firm, thus tending disproportionally to reduce the volume of foreign investment in that country. In addition, the relative unattractiveness of such a country also tends to mean that the local government's bargaining leverage with the international corporation is not strong. As a result the host country could not expect decisively to influence either the sectoral distribution of capital inflows or the extent to which the technology embodied in such flows were employment creating. Furthermore argues Evans, even where dependent development does occur "the consequence of industrializing on the basis of this logic is the exclusion of most of the population from the potential benefits of industrialization."[13]

With respect to the Caribbean, the Lewis strategy, as implemented, was not without some degree of success. As hypothesized by Evans, however, by no means was this process as successful as it had been in the much larger Brazil. Jamaica and Trinidad and Tobago were the recipients of substantial amounts of manufacturing investment during the 1950s and 1960s. Because of this the structures of their economies underwent a substantial degree of change with manufacturing assuming increased importance. Similarly the level of per capita output rose significantly in both countries, raising the level of production per capita substantially above that of the world's poorest nations. Other parts of the region, however, did not fare as well, with the level of manufacturing investment in Barbados and Guyana far below that in Trinidad and Tobago and Jamaica.

Between 1950 and 1968 Jamaica's real gross domestic product increased from $171.00 (J) to $549.20 (J), an average annual increase of 6.7 percent. Manufacturing output grew at a rate even more rapid than that of the overall economy. Between these same years this sector's percentage contribution to output increased from 13.9 to 16.2 percent. By 1968, manufacturing in Jamaica had become that country's single most important economic sector.[14] A similar pattern prevailed in Trinidad and Tobago. Between 1951 and 1961 the average annual rate of growth of real gross domestic product was 8.5 percent.[15] This growth rate decelerated in the 1960s but, even so, real per capita domestic product increased by about 2.3 percent per year between 1963 and 1968. During these years alone exports of manufactured goods doubled, substantially increasing this sector's contribution to output.[16]

Despite these impressive growth rates, however, there can be little doubt that the strategy of "industrialization by invitation" proved disappointing. The experiences of both Jamaica and Trinidad and Tobago suggest that even success in attracting capital imports may not have much impact on the problems of unemployment and poverty. Thus in Trinidad and Tobago, unemployment in 1966 stood at 14 percent. Comparable levels of unemployment existed elsewhere in the region. In April

1966, the unemployment rate in Barbados was 13 percent, in Guyana it was estimated at 20.9 percent in 1965, and in Jamaica in 1967 at 18 percent.[17] In 1970, Jack Harewood estimated unemployment in the region as a whole at between 15 and 25 percent. In addition, he estimates that in Trinidad and Tobago, the only country for which data allowed such an estimate, underemployment came to 37 percent.[18]

The case is similar with respect to the persistence of poverty. Harewood has noted that in all likelihood

> the greatest poverty is to be found in those households where there is no one capable of being in the labor force or else in households where adults of working age . . . eke out an existence by employing themselves in petty jobs and self-employment of a kind that brings only the barest minimum income.[19]

It appears likely that the number of such households increased during this period. Between 1946 and 1960 in every territory studied, labor force participation rates actually declined.[20] This in combination with the rising unemployment rate suggests the likelihood that the percentage of poverty-stricken households may have increased during this time period. At the very least it can be said that the success achieved in industrialization in this period did not substantially improve the living standards of a large majority of the region's population. In this regard therefore the experience in the Caribbean tends to support Evans' view of the "exclusionary" tendencies of dependent development.

In addition to its failure to resolve the problems of poverty and unemployment, the strategy of dependent development in the Caribbean raised problems in the realm of politics and class rule. The strategy was implemented in the West Indies just as the process of decolonization was undertaken. It was thus essayed at a time when the class structures of the countries of the region were greatly in flux. Specifically in many cases an indigenous ruling class had not yet fully established itself. Local ruling elites had as yet failed to secure for themselves an economic foundation to complement their political authority, a weakness which was reenforced by the dependency strategy itself. As a result the West Indian situation was unlike that of Brazil where a stable class alliance including local business people was feasible.

Fundamentally the problem is that dependency implies a continued strong expatriate influence in society, an imposition which may be harmful to the interests of a fledgling ruling class. Where the local governing authorities are weak, dependency implies a structural incapacity for such an elite to alleviate economic problems. Since economic decision-making powers reside outside the region, no local authority possesses the capacity to influence decisively the course of the domestic economy. In turn this raises the possibility of a potentially dangerous inability to defuse the social tensions associated with economic difficulties. This weakness resides precisely in the fact that so long as dependency on foreign capital persists, local elites will be rooted institutionally only very marginally in the local economy. For such leaders one of the reasons dependency is unsatisfactory is that it paralyzes their efforts to address potentially threatening tension creating problems.

This inability to exercise influence on the economy is made graphic in Charles C. Moskos Jr.'s data on the Caribbean region's political and labor union leaders in the early 1960s. Of the forty-six individuals whom he interviewed, only three owned large businesses and one owned a large plantation. Two-thirds of the forty-six were barristers, teachers, doctors, dentists, small business owners or held salaried white-collar jobs. The remaining twelve of the forty-six were either manual laborers or farmers.[21] What these data suggest is that the typical West Indian political leader was only tangentially related to the region's centers of production. Only a handful were actually involved in managerial roles and able directly to influence decisions to increase or reduce production. Political leaders in the region, thus, were only weakly rooted in those sectors of society where the fundamental and basic economic decisions – decisions related to output and employment – were made.

The unsatisfactory nature of dependent development thus was experienced at all levels of West Indian society. Preeminently, the pressure for change was generated by the poor and the unemployed. They personally experienced the failure of the dependent development approach and reacted with both parliamentary and extra-parliamentary pressures. But in addition, an interest in change also tended to be present among sections of the region's political elite. The latter's economic nationalism – their desire to generate an economic base over which they possessed jurisdiction – in part was in reaction to the pressure they felt from the lower classes in society.[22] Threatened from below, but incapable of exercising much leverage over foreign firms, they searched for a new structure of economic activity out of political self-defense. Whatever the motivation, however, by the 1970s a powerful multiclass convergence of views on the necessity for a change in economic strategy had developed.

NOTES

1. Gordon K. Lewis, *The Growth of the Modern West Indies* (New York: Monthly Review Press, 1968), p. 88.
2. Great Britain, West India Royal Commission, *Report* CMD, 6607 (London HMSO: 1945), pp. 247, 252, 278.
3. W. Arthur Lewis, "The Industrialization of the British West Indies," *Caribbean Economic Review*, Vol. 2, 1950, pp. 1–61.
4. Lewis, "Industrialization of British West Indies," pp. 31, 38, 40.
5. Lewis, "Industrialization of British West Indies," pp. 31, 44–45, 46, 48–49.
6. Gunnar Myrdal, *Economic Theory and Underdeveloped Regions* (New York: Harper & Row, 1957).
7. F. H. Cardoso, "Notas sobre o Estado Atual Dos Estudos Sobre Dependencia," in Frank Bonilla and Robert Girling, eds., *Structures of Dependency* (Nairobi, California, 1973), p. 15.
8. F. H. Cardoso, "Imperialism and Dependency in Latin America," in Bonilla and Girling, eds., *Structures of Dependency*, p. 11.
9. Cardoso, "Notas Sobre," p. 16.
10. Peter Evans, *Dependent Development: The Alliance of Multinational, State and Local Capital in Brazil* (Princeton: Princeton University Press, 1979), p. 44.
11. Evans, *Dependent Development*, p. 44.
12. Evans, *Dependent Development*, p. 272.
13. Evans, *Dependent Development*, p. 33, 12.
14. Owen Jefferson, *The Post-War Economic Development of Jamaica* (Jamaica: Institute of Social and Economic Research, University of the West Indies, 1972), pp. 44–45, 48.
15. Selwyn Ryan, "Restructuring the Trinidad Economy," in Norman Girvan and Owen Jefferson, eds., *Readings in the Political Economy of the Caribbean* (Jamaica: New World Group Ltd., 1961), p. 187.
16. Government of Trinidad and Tobago, *Third Five Year Plan 1969–1973*, p. 423.
17. Jack Harewood, "The Under-Utilization of Available Human Resources," in Jack Harewood, ed., *Human Resources in the Commonwealth Caribbean* (Trinidad: Institution of Social and Economic Research, University of the West Indies, 1970), p. 5.

18. Jack Harewood, "West Indian People," in G. Beckford, ed., *Caribbean Economy: Dependence and Backwardness* (Jamaica: Institute of Social and Economic Research, University of the West Indies, 1975), p. 14.
19. Harewood, "West Indian People," p. 18.
20. Carmen McFarlane, "The Employment Situation in Overpopulated Territories in the Commonwealth Caribbean," in Jack Harewood, ed., *Human Resources* in the Commonwealth Caribbean, pp. 4–12.
21. Calculated from Charles C. Moskos Jr., *The Sociology of Political Independence* (Cambridge: Schenkman Publishing Company, 1967), Table 4, p. 33.
22. For an interesting discussion of the elite's perception of the attitudes of the urban poor in Jamaica in the early 1960s, see James A. Mau, "The Threatening Masses: Myth or Reality?" in F. M. Andic and T. C. Mathews, eds., *The Caribbean in Transition* (Rio Piedras: Institute of Caribbean Studies, University of Puerto Rico, 1965), pp. 258–270.

Chapter 6

Alternatives to Dependency

In one respect there were similarities in the responses of Jamaica, Guyana and Trinidad and Tobago to the dependency of the 1950s and 1960s. Everywhere in the region local political leaders moved to enhance the role of the government in the economy. Such a common movement is not really surprising. Any governmental leadership, perceiving itself threatened by a hostile population might very well think in terms of moving in the direction of an increased importance for the public sector in order to alleviate this hostility. This might especially be the case where, as in the Caribbean, the governing elite does not own a substantial share of the commercial and business enterprises and therefore does not possess a substantial personal stake in the well-being of the private sector in the economy.

Specific political and social circumstances affected the ideological defense which was mounted to justify the enhanced role for the state. In Guyana, the nationalist turn in economic policymaking took the form of the adoption of a socialist ideology by the dominant party. The political circumstances of Trinidad and Tobago, as well as the fact that the country was the beneficiary of petro-dollars, meant that the turn to nationalism there was less ideological. But even in Trinidad and Tobago, the increase in the direct participation of the government in the economy was extensive. Indeed, the extent of government economic control through direct and partial ownership of enterprises was more extensive in the latter than it was in Michael Manley's "socialist" Jamaica. The point is that the expansion of the public sector in Caribbean countries – irrespective of ideology – was the means by which the political elites attempted to gain increased control of the local economy, a pattern of control which was not available to it in the full expression of dependency.

The tendency towards government ownership of productive

enterprises thus represents the reaction of the post-colonial political elites to the failure of the free-market dependent-development economic strategy. The latter, while successful in raising income levels and in promoting industrialization in at least some countries, failed in important areas of concern to local policymakers. It failed to provide the governing class with adequate instruments to ease the pressures associated with widespread poverty and unemployment. It thus failed to provide an economic dimension to the authority of this class. The result was an effort to correct this deficiency by vesting economic authority as well as political control in the hands of officials in government.

But aside from this enhanced role for government the three largest countries of the English-speaking Caribbean followed divergent paths. On the one hand there was an attempt by Jamaica and Guyana to reduce their dependency and embark upon a more self-reliant path of development. In Guyana this took the form of extensive nationalizations, while in Jamaica democratic socialism allowed the private sector to retain a central role in the economy. On the other hand, Trinidad, benefitting from its position as a petroleum producer attempted to accelerate its industrialization by attracting private foreign investment to join with the Trinidad government in joint ventures. In this chapter we discuss the circumstances which lead Jamaica and Guyana to follow the more autonomous model of growth and the requirements which must be satisfied if a decisive break with dependency is to be achieved.

In both Jamaica and Guyana major choice points were reached in the early 1970s. Throughout the 1960s in Guyana the strategy of dependent development had been an almost total failure. It had been successful in attracting almost no investment capital in manufacturing. Only a limited amount of clothing and footware made the list of exports from the country. Indeed, in its annual economic survey the government in 1973 itself complained that "despite numerous incentives and encouragement in the form of tax holidays and duty free concessions, the sector remains dormant with very little expansion and diversification."[1] In Jamaica, as we have seen, this strategy was not as complete a failure. By the end of the 1960s the list of manufactured goods produced in the country was impressively large including metal products, chemicals, plastics, containers, electrical goods, clothing and leather products. Even so, however, the inflow of capital was neither large enough, nor sufficiently job-creating to absorb more than a small fraction of Jamaica's growing labor force. As a result, festering problems of poverty and unemployment prevailed despite the reality of substantial economic expansion.[2]

Finally, in neither country did the bauxite sector provide much of a stimulus to industrialization. Here again, as with Jamaican manufacturing, the problem was that the aluminum firms tended to export the raw material to locations closer to the ultimate market before processing it. Thus the potential for an integrated set of manufacturing industries based on aluminum was denied the region. In effect, the absence of local control over the use of the domestic raw material precluded the development of industries around bauxite.[3]

By the 1970s, then, the governments of Jamaica and Guyana were under increasing pressure to do something about their economies. These pressures were especially manifest in elections held in 1972 and 1973, respectively. In its election campaign, their opposition party, the People's National Party, headed by Michael Manley, promised "power to the people." It is significant, however, that the party in the 1972 election did not project a left-wing or socialist political line. Indeed, one close observer of the election noted that "on election day, the two parties entered the contest with no significant differences in policy. . . . " Nevertheless, the overwhelming victory given to Manley's party is suggestive of the deep dissatisfaction that prvailed in the country, and this same observer notes that the previous ruling party "may well have been overwhelmed by the imperative of change."[4]

In Guyana, the political situation was quite different. Each of the two major political parties had come to represent one of the major ethnic groups in the country: the ruling People's National Congress (PNC) representing the descendants of the former African slaves and the People's Progressive Party (PPP) the East Indian community. But superimposed on the racial politics of the nation was an ideological dimension, especially as represented by the PPP, which called itself a Marxist-Leninist party and had long been associated with socialist politics.

There was never much doubt that, by virtue of its control over the country's electoral machinery, the PNC was to be returned to office in the 1973 election. What may have surprised the party, however, was that it received only limited support in one of the party's areas of traditional strength, Georgetown. This limited support took the form of a low voter turnout in "safe" electoral districts.[5] It is quite conceivable, given some concurrent ideological defections from the party, that the government of Forbes Burnham during this period was itself sensitive to the inadequacy of the economic policies currently in force.

The pressure for change in the 1972 and 1973 elections was dramatically reinforced in 1973–74, a year of substantial inflation caused at least in part by the new found market power of the petroleum producing countries. In 1974 alone, the urban consumer price index increased by an estimated 20 percent in Guyana, a figure that could not help but substantially reduce living standards in the country. A similar, even larger, price inflation was experienced in Jamaica. Furthermore, the Jamaican economy was hurt by depressed markets for bauxite and alumium and the severe recession experienced that year in the world economy. The result was a sharp decline in new foreign investment in the country and the likelihood that unemployment would increase substantially even as prices mounted.[7] In short, not only had the prevailing economic strategy of foreign investment failed in Guyana to stimulate economic development, but also the vulnerability of the dependent economies of both countries to uncontrolled outside shocks had been made manifest.

Within the year, the governments of both Michael Manley and Forbes Burnham responded to these developments by issuing new policy statements. In both cases, the governments declared their intention to institute policies to achieve socialism. In Guyana, the PNC had already declared itself to be a socialist party in a new constitution drafted in December 1973. However, the content of this position was more fully articulated in an address by Burnham in December 1974 that has since come to be known as the "Declaration of Sophia." According to this document, the PNC was a socialist party and its intention was to lead Guyana to socialism. In this regard the party affirmed the desirability of a "tri-sectoral" economy in which a cooperative sector stood alongside the public and private sectors. The "Declaration of Sophia," however, was careful to delimit the role of private foreign investment in Guyana. It assured that "private investment from abroad is welcome in specific fields in consortium with government and/or cooperatives." It added as a proviso, however, that "in each case governments and/or cooperatives should hold majority equity and real control."[8]

A similar posture was adopted by the Manley government in Jamaica. In its document, "Democratic Socialism for Jamaica," the PNP government declared that "we are constructing our own model of Socialism." The Jamaican version of socialism provided wider latitude to private and foreign investment than did the Guyanese. Nonetheless, the position articulated restricted the freedom of private investors to search out profit-making opportunities. The government stated that it

> recognized that there is a legitimate place in the society for the businessman who combines creativity and initiative in providing goods and services of good quality and at reasonable prices which people need.

Nonetheless, under socialism,

> the Private Businessman is expected to work within the bonds of the National interest and the rights of the people [and therefore] economic activity must . . . be directed and regulated by the government to ensure basic needs of all the people are met.

Specifically, foreign investment was welcome in Jamaica but only if "it is willing to enter into partnership with local private interests, the government or both, as may be required by the Government of Jamaica."[9]

Subsequent experience revealed that these policy declarations were not merely rhetorical statements. The Guyanese government moved actively to expand the public sector at the expense of private interests. With the nationalization of Bookers Brothers and the sugar industry in May 1976 there remained very little in the economy that was not either owned or controlled by government. In Jamaica, the pace of nationalization was slower. Nonetheless, the government purchased part of the bauxite sector, embarked upon a significant land-reform program, came to own a substantial fraction of the tourist industry's capacity, and expanded the welfare and minimum wage laws in the country. In 1977 it initially resisted intense International Monetary Fund (IMF) pressure to devalue the Jamaican dollar by 40 percent, the condition set by the IMF before providing aid for the country's balance-of-payments deficit. In 1980 it rejected terms demanded by the IMF for a renewal of the loan program.[10] Relevant too are the foreign policy stances adopted by these countries. To a rather surprising extent both Jamaica and Guyana modified their foreign policies and aimed at closer relations with socialist countries in general and with Cuba in particular. The effect of this orientation was to create tensions with the United States.

In this context, however, two analytic problems suggest themselves. The first is the need to identify what alternatives are available to poor countries which attempt to reduce their dependency. The second is the question of the requisites of success in implementing such an alternative. This second issue is of particular importance in a context like that of Jamaica and Guyana where the shift in development strategy was announced without a social revolution and indeed in the absence of significant changes in personnel in the governing regimes of these countries. The question which arises here is whether the state, broadly understood in the Marxist sense, can be expected successfully to make the transition from the implementation of one approach to development to an entirely different method.

In principle it is possible to model a viable alternative to dependent capitalist development. A country can disengage from world capitalism and seek out the means to achieve increased output from sources other than multinational corporations. When this is done there must be a shift from efforts to tap external sources of technology, capital and management. Instead of these, sources of growth must be located domestically. With this self-centered approach, therefore, an enormously increased burden is placed on local leadership. For with dependency the central problem of development – the application of advancing technology to production – rests in the hands of expatriate firms. The principal responsibility of local political leaders is merely to provide the context in which such firms can function efficiently. With self-reliance, the central resource mobilizing function is shifted to local hands and the burden of achieving productive efficiency becomes located domestically. The central question which arises in the self-reliant approach is whether indigenous sources of wealth can be identified and whether a shift to local decision-makers can be achieved successfully.

Generally it is to agriculture that a country must look if it is to achieve self-reliant growth. There are two reasons for this. First, if external sources of investment are to be minimized, then it can only be from the wealth produced in the country that new investment can be financed. But since in poor countries agriculture is the dominant indigenous industry it is from the rural areas that the nation must obtain the resources to create new industries. The second reason centers on the question of foreign exchange. At the level of economic development at which the Caribbean finds itself, new equipment and capital goods must be purchased from abroad, if only to establish a local capital goods industry. But for such imports to be purchased from abroad foreign exchange must be available. That, in turn, once again implies the need to expand agricultural output. For expanded agricultural output could allow a country either to cut down on its food import bill or to expand its volume of agricultural exports. In either case additional foreign exchange would be available to help promote the industrialization process.

What all of this means is that for a country engaged in an effort to achieve autonomous development a failure to expand agricultural output substantially can have important negative consequences. Stagnating output will hinder a country's ability to create new industries. Similarly a failure to achieve agricultural dynamism will constrain a nation's ability to import essential capital goods. Thus in autonomous development the experience of agriculture governs the performance of the economy as a whole. As a result a successful break with dependency requires an expanding and prosperous agricultural sector.

The legacy of the plantation economy in the region, however, has made it extremely difficult to accomplish the goal of agricultural modernization. For what emerged in its aftermath was an agricultural sector in which land ownership was extremely concentrated. This meant that for the bulk of the farmers, the scale of their operation was too small to facilitate technological progress. Modern capital equipment could not be employed without encountering serious problems of underutilization. In any case the limited resources available to such farmers increased their aversion to risk and encouraged technologically conservative behavior. At the other end of the spectrum crop choice inflexibility and land underutilization were characteristic of the large farms. The first was especially the case where local farms were part of a vertically integrated process extending from cultivation to food marketing. In such a circumstance even a decrease in price did not encourage crop diversification because of the "downstream" commitments of the firm.[11] But at the same time unutilized land held in reserve was a rational response to the possibility of expanding markets in the future. It is clear, however, the rigidities in crop choice and use of less land than is available comes at a high price for a country which needs to earn as much as possible from its agricultural sector as a means to achieve economic development. In these circumstances output will neither be as large as it could be nor be concentrated in the most lucrative crops. But given the centrality of agriculture to autonomous development the income foregone in these ways will have important negative implications for the entire development process.

The actual pattern of land ownership in Jamaica in the late 1960s is provided in Table 6.1. There it is revealed that there were in excess of 150,000 farms under 5 acres, while there were 293 farms in excess of 500 acres. The latter representing less than 0.2 percent of all farms in the country occupied 45 percent of all farm land. The small farms, representing almost 80 percent of all units, occupied about 15 percent of farm land. It should be noted that these data, illustrating extreme land concentration, take no account of the fact that the quality of the land in large holdings was far superior to that of the small farmers.[12]

Though most data for Guyana are quite dated, the same general pattern prevailed in that country until the nationalization of the sugar industry occurred in 1976. Almost one-half of the farms in Guyana were between one and five acres in 1953.[13] At the time of the nationalization, the two firms which owned the sugar industry occupied a little less than one-third of the acreage cultivated in the country. As was the case in Jamaica,

Table 6.1
STRUCTURE OF AGRICULTURE IN JAMAICA, 1968–1969

	Farm Size	
	Less than 5 Acres	More than 500 Acres
Number	151,705	293
Percentage of all farms	78.6	0.2
Percentage of all acreage in cultivation	14.9	44.9

Revised and calculated from the source: George L. Beckford, "Caribbean Rural Economy," in George L. Beckford, ed., *Caribbean Economy* (Jamaica: Institute of Social and Economic Research, 1975), p. 87; and Don Robothom, "Agrarian Relations in Jamaica," in Carl Stone and Aggrey Brown, eds., *Essays on Power and Change in Jamaica* (Jamaica: University of the West Indies, 1976), p. 121.

these plantation lands were the most fertile in the country, a result of the fact that substantial investment in drainage and irrigation had been made in them, while few water control facilities were available on nonplantation land.

With the inception of efforts to achieve autonomous growth in Jamaica and Guyana in the 1970s, these landholding patterns clearly suggest that there was a need for a program of land reform. Given the structure of land ownership in these countries, it was extremely unlikely that without major structural changes agricultural modernization could be achieved. Not until the difficulties caused by an underfinanced peasantry and the underutilization of land and excessive rigidities in output mix associated with the very large farms were overcome could agriculture be expected to contribute successfully to the new development effort. Land reform was a precondition for autonomous growth.

Two competing models of how to accomplish the goal of growth-promoting land reform have been suggested by West Indian economists. George Beckford has argued for a program which he calls "integral land reform." In this, holdings of five to twenty-five acres will be allocated to the rural peasantry. He argues that since peasants can be relied upon to be more innovative and to cultivate their land more intensively than large landholders, such a redistribution will result in expanded agricultural output. This is especially likely if, as he advocates, this land redistribution occurs at the same time that reforms are implemented with regard to the extension of credit, technical assistance, seed and fertilizer availability, and marketing outlets. Such a program, argues Beckford, will contribute to the process by which "improvements in the economic and social welfare of people are consistently achieved over time."[14]

With a similar concern Clive Y. Thomas has called for a program of agricultural collectivization, though carefully noting that this program should be carried out only with the willing compliance of the peasants themselves. It is only with large scale units of production, larger than those associated with a peasantry, argues Thomas, that modern and technologically progressive inputs can be employed in agriculture. Thus it is that Thomas argues that agriculture's contribution to autonomous growth requires a collectivized and cooperative agricultural sector.[15]

In fact, neither Thomas' nor Beckford's approach is problem free. Thomas, for his part, does not satisfactorily answer the question of what to do if the peasantry resists collectivization, as he, himself, concedes it might. He writes, for example, that peasants frequently see the ending of exploitation as occurring "by way of greater security of private tenure and real income, both of which the peasant believes can only follow from an expansion of holding size and from the preservation and extension of unrestricted rights to the use and disposal of land." But at the same time he resists imposing collectivization on an unwilling peasantry. He notes that the experiences of the Soviet Union "have shown that if democracy is not preserved in the rural areas the peasantry will be driven to retaliation and to the sabotage of the transition efforts."[16] The problem is that Thomas does not reconcile his commitment to democracy and voluntarism with the possibility that the farming community might resist collectivization. He does not indicate how to escape or at least soften the dilemma which might arise when such an agricultural reorganization is attempted. In particular he does not indicate the relative weights which should be attached to democracy and collectivization respectively or the priority which should be attached to each. As a result of this gap, a policy vacuum appears in his approach at precisely a critical moment – missing is the answer to what the political leadership should do to attain its goals and what limits it should respect in this pursuit.

Beckford's approach contains a different problem. The political strength of his model is that in it the farmers obtain the land, credit and technical assistance which they desire. But its weakness stems from the unproved assumption contained in it that when "integral land reform" is implemented, technological dynamism will result. The latter is essential if the model of autonomous development is to be successful. But on both empirical and analytic grounds, there is grave cause for concern that a peasant-based agricultural community will be able to produce the kind of agricultural modernization essential for this approach.

The basis for Beckford's belief that a peasantry can carry such a burden are empirical studies which show that yields per acre are higher on small scale farms than on large sacle units of production. Statistical analyses by Cline are cited in this regard as are data which indicate that productivity for all inputs, not just land, are relatively high on peasant farms.[17] The problem is, however, that this is not the kind of evidence which is needed to make the point that a peasantry is competent to produce technological dynamism. For the data reported in these studies are concerned with the intensity of factor use, holding time constant. But the problem of technological dynamism is centered on the introduction of new methods of production and crops with the passage of time. Beckford himself acknowledges that "empirical evidence is weakest in respect of the relationships between technical change and land reform."[18] This weakness makes it impossible for Beckford to refute Thomas' contention that modern agriculture requires units of production "which are larger than is generally available to peasants."[19]

It is obvious that the disagreement between Thomas and Beckford cannot be resolved simply through debate and discussion. There are simply too many variables which cannot be sufficiently specified in each approach to be able to be certain that either is capable of both satisfying the desires of the rural population and the requirements of economic development. What this suggests is that a government in power and committed to a model of autonomous development will probably have to engage in an extended period of experimentation before a satisfactory agricultural structure can be created.

But the consensus which Beckford and Thomas share is also important. For there is agreement that there must be a reorganization of the agrarian structure and an elimination of the private concentration of land ownership before the constraints to expanded output can be removed. In addition Beckford and Thomas agree that the new organizational form adopted in the countryside must at once capture the good will of the rural community, while at the same time facilitating the introduction of new productivity raising methods of production. In short, in the self-reliant approach to development a close collaborative relationship between the government and the farming community is necessary. Only by involving rural workers and farmers in decisions with regard to organizational forms can government hope to tap and maintain the good will of these groups. The presence of such good will is the necessary condition which has to be satisfied if a mututally acceptable structure of farming is ultimately to be created.

But it is precisely because of the centrality of agricultural reform in autonomous development that questions can be raised about the feasibility of this approach. For what is fundamental to this strategy is the capacity of the political leadership of the country to mobilize the rural community and guide its reorganization. And for that capacity to be present, leadership must possess both a strong organizational base and a fund of good will among the rural population. The paradox, however, is that the regimes in the region interested in implementing self-reliant growth – the Manley government in Jamaica and the Burnham government in Guyana – were both urban dominated with respect to their constituencies and interests. Furthermore in Guyana the rural/urban difference is compounded by an important racial fissure. Neither government, therefore, was well positioned to exercise the kind of leadership necessary to transform the social structure of the countryside. Indeed for both regimes there was the risk that they would experience opposition on two fronts in their efforts to implement self-reliance. Resistance might be encountered from their own constituents eager to speed and secure the benefits of economic advance for themselves or resistance might be generated from the rural community, distrustful of change emanating from what is perceived as an alien government.

It follows from this that only if the peasantry and its representatives are included in the governing regimes in the area is it possible to envision the tensions and conflicts arising from autonomous growth being accommodated. Even then, there is no doubt that the strains, such a rural/urban, worker/farmer coalition will experience will be substantial.

The issues raised by Thomas and Beckford thus have an important political dimension. If, as is likely, the peasants prefer maintaining their hold on the land, but rapid economic development requires some form of centralization or collectivization, then it is in the political realm that this conflict will have to be resolved. What will be required is that the representatives of each side of this urban/rural division recognize the good will of the other and the fact that mutual gain can be accomplished only through accommodation. Certainly such a political good will is not impossible to envision. But what it requires is precisely a commodity which has not been notably present in the region to date: a willingness to share power in decision-making with potential antagonists.

NOTES

1. Ministry of Economic Development, *Economic Survey of Guyana, 1973*, p. 40.
2. R. K. Girling, "Technology and Dependent Development in Jamaica," *Social and Economic Studies* 25, 2 (June 1977):169.
3. See Norman Girvan, *Foreign Capital and Economic Underdevelopment in Jamaica* (Jamaica: Institute of Social and Economic Research, University of the West Indies, 1971).
4. Olive Senior, *The Message Is Change: A Perspective on the 1972 General Elections* (Kingston: Kingston Publisher Ltd., 1972), pp. 3, 19.

5. Voter participation rates in the eight electoral districts of Greater Georgetown were lower than in all other electoral districts in the country.
6. Bank of Guyana, *Economic Bulletin No. 9* (Georgetown, October 1975), p. 75.
7. *Economic and Social Survey, Jamaica*, 1975.
8. "Declaration of Sophia" (Address by the Leader of the People's National Congress, Prime Minister Forbes Burnham, at a Special Congress to Mark the Tenth Anniversary of the PNC in Government, December 14, 1974), p. 22.
9. *Democratic Socialism for Jamaica* (Kingston: The Agency for Public Information, n.d.), pp. 1, 3.
10. For the government's position on this see Saul Landau, "Jamaica's Hot Politics," *Mother Jones*, Vol. V, No. VIII, Sept./Oct. 1980.
11. Malcolm Cross, *Urbanization and Urban Growth in the Caribbean. An Essay on Social Change in Dependent Societies* (New York: Cambridge University Press, 1979), p. 35.
12. George L. Beckford, "Caribbean Rural Economy," in George L. Beckford, ed., *Caribbean Economy* (Jamaica: Institute of Social and Economic Research, University of the West Indies, 1975), p. 86.
13. O. P. Blaich, *Agriculture in British Guiana*, Census 1952, Vol. I, No. 1, p. 17.
14. George L. Beckford, "Land Reform for the Betterment of Caribbean Peoples," *Proceedings of the 7th West Indies Agricultural Economics Conference*, Grand Anse, Grenada, 1972, p. 26.
15. Clive Y. Thomas, *Dependence and Transformation: The Economics of the Transition to Socialism* (New York: Monthly Review Press, 1974), p. 153.
16. Thomas, *Dependence and Transformation*, pp. 162, 164.
17. In this regard Beckford cites William R. Cline, *Economic Consequences of a Land Reform in Brazil* (Amsterdam, 1970). Since the publication of Beckford's article a fuller statement of this point of view has appeared in R. Albert Berry and William R. Cline, *Agrarian Structure and Productivity in Developing Countries* (Baltimore and London: The Johns Hopkins University Press, 1979).
18. Beckford, "Land Reform for the Betterment of Caribbean Peoples," p. 29.
19. Thomas, *Dependence and Transformation*, p. 153.

Chapter 7

Agrarian Reform in Cuba

The one place in the Caribbean where the kind of agricultural reform discussed by George Beckford and Clive Thomas has been implemented is Cuba. The initiation of an agrarian reform program in Cuba was not as difficult as it was in the rest of the region since, as Arthur MacEwan writes, the Cuban leaders saw themselves as having "firm roots and strong political support in the countryside."[1] The gap between the urban political leadership and the predominantly rural population, characteristic of the English-speaking Caribbean was only minimally present in Cuba. At the same time the Cuban Revolutionary leadership was committed to a radical reconstruction of the country's social structure. Thus the land reform undertaken in that country comes close to providing a test case of what a land reform program might look like and the problems it might encounter if it were attempted in a country like Jamaica, Trinidad and Tobago, Barbados or Guyana. It must be emphasized that what follows does not pretend to be a full discussion of Cuba's economic performance since 1959. Rather it is an effort to explore those elements of its agrarian reform experience which might be relevant if a comparable effort were tried elsewhere in the region.

The Cuba agrarian reform occurred in two stages. The first was accomplished in May of 1959 with the passage of the first agrarian reform law. With this, large holdings, those in excess of 402.3 hectares, were prohibited. Estates confiscated under this law were not to be broken up and redistributed but were to be worked as cooperatives. Other, non-estate land was to be redistributed and was to be given to individual cultivators up to a maximum of 67 hectares and in no case below 27 hectares.

But it was the second agrarian reform act, implemented in October 1963, which provided the framework which governed subsequent Cuban agriculture development. With this act the maximum an individual farmer could cultivate was reduced to 67 hectares and expropriated land was consolidated in state farms. After 1963 about 3/4 of the nation's total and about 3/5 of its cultivated land was in the public sector. Thus the 1963 act differed from the 1959 reform in two important ways. The maximum size of private holdings was severely reduced and the organizational form for the land which had been taken over was changed from cooperatives to state farms.[2]

In both of these agrarian reforms it is obvious that the Cubans were grappling with the same kinds of issues discussed by Beckford and Thomas. Having broken up the very large concentrations of land-holding, the Cubans had to address the questions of to whom, in what size allotments, and under what institutional arrangements this land should be reallocated. At the same time, however, even under the second agrarian reform the private sector was not entirely eliminated. Even as state controlled acreage increased enormously, the number of relatively small-scale farms also increased. By 1963 compared to 1959 the number of peasant farms had increased from about 40,000 to 45,000 to 160,000 private farms.[3] In effect a dual agricultural structure was created with the dominant organizational form corresponding to Thomas' model, but a not insignificant sector approximating the position adopted by Beckford.

As we have argued, the primary criterion against which the effectiveness of an agrarian reform must be measured is its role in stimulating production. Non-dependent development requires that agricultural production be buoyant. But such a program as well can be seen to have a welfare effect, especially with regard to the distribution of income. There is no doubt that the Cuban agrarian reform narrowed considerably the contry's distribution of income. MacEwan emphasizes that poverty in pre-Revolutionary Cuba had been concentrated in the countryside.[4] Rural incomes increased under the reform program as small farmers gained access to land and also because with the new law rental payments were reduced. At the same time the creation of state farms allowed the government to offer employment virtually to all rural workers. The result of these income raising and employment creating programs was to shift income to the countryside and as a consequence attack an important source of inequality in the country.

The Cuban agrarian reform experience, however, is much less impressive when it is measured against the criterion of encouraging expanded output. Tables 7.1 and 7.2 show output trends for four major crops for the period from the early 1960's either through 1973 or 1974. In no case is it possible to claim a substantial upward trend in output. Similarly, a composite index of per capita agricultural output, including sugar, reveals no positive trend in production (Table 7.3). Thus in the aggregate there is no evidence to indicate that the agrarian reform program in Cuba unleashed the kind of increased output essential for the pattern of development that country was pursing.

Table 7.1

COLLECTION OF GRAINS AND TUBERS BY SECTOR OF ORIGIN, 1962–74 (THOUSAND METRIC TONS)

	Grains				Tubers			
	Total	Private	Public	% Public	Total	Private	Public	% Public
1962	340.2	140.6	199.6	58.7	345.2	249.8	95.4	27.6
1963	319.7	116.5	203.2	63.6	429.7	288.5	141.2	32.9
1964	174.6	52.2	122.4	70.1	440.6	261.0	179.6	40.8
1965	82.3	39.0	43.3	52.6	402.2	255.5	176.7	43.9
1966	96.6	32.6	64.0	66.3	545.9	252.8	293.1	43.7
1967	117.1	31.4	85.7	73.2	393.5	171.8	221.7	56.3
1968	111.5	20.0	91.5	82.1	410.5	160.3	250.2	61.0
1969	189.3	16.2	178.3	94.2	326.2	130.8	195.4	60.0
1970	299.4	11.0	288.4	96.3	196.7	75.3	121.4	61.7
1971	297.2	15.1	282.1	94.9	239.3	82.6	156.7	65.5
1972	251.0	19.2	231.8	92.4	383.5	168.1	215.4	56.2
1973	244.0	13.7	230.3	94.4	397.5	181.9	215.6	54.2
1974	347.7	NA	NA	–	289.5	NA	NA	–

Revised and calculated from the source: Arthur MacEwan, "Cuban Agriculture and Development: Contradictionsand Progress," p. 348, 361.

Table 7.2

COLLECTION OF VEGETABLES AND FRUITS BY SECTOR OF ORIGIN, 1962–74 (THOUSAND METRIC TONS)

	Vegetables				Fruits			
	Total	Private	Public	% Public	Total	Private	Public	% Public
1962	–	–	–	–	–	–	–	–
1963	–	–	–	–	365.6	268.9	96.7	26.4
1964	195.0	142.4	52.6	27.0	291.7	184.0	107.7	36.9
1965	220.4	161.2	59.2	26.9	325.4	224.9	100.5	31.3
1966	230.9	162.4	68.5	29.7	321.3	217.7	103.6	32.2
1967	282.7	188.4	94.3	33.4	318.1	213.1	105.0	33.0
1968	216.7	138.7	78.0	36.0	385.0	240.1	144.9	37.6
1969	126.7	82.1	44.6	35.2	297.4	171.0	126.4	42.5
1970	136.2	62.7	73.5	54.0	289.7	125.7	164.0	56.6
1971	172.2	74.0	98.2	57.0	296.9	130.1	166.8	56.2
1972	150.0	63.3	86.7	57.8	372.4	161.7	210.7	56.6
1973	239.8	123.6	116.2	48.5	434.0	207.9	226.1	52.1
1974	265.9	NA	NA	–	463.4	NA	NA	–

Revised and calculated from the source: See Table 7.1.

Table 7.3

INDEX OF CUBAN AGRICULTURAL PRODUCTION AND AGRICULTURAL PRODUCTION PER CAPITA, 1966–77

1969–71 = 100	Agriculture	Agriculture per capita
1966	77	83
1967	92	97
1968	89	92
1969	86	88
1970	122	122
1971	93	91
1972	86	83
1973	90	85
1974	93	86
1975	98	89
1976	97	86
1977	103	90

Revised and calculated from the source: James W. Wilkie, *Statistical Abstract of Latin America* (Los Angeles: UCLA Latin American Center Publication, 1980).

Table 7.1 and 7.2 do however reveal an important trend in food crop production. While output for fruits, vegetables, grains and tubers remained about stable through the mid 1970's, in all crops the public share of this production increased at the expense of private sector production. In the case of grain the public sector share increased from about 3/5 to virtually the entire output while for the other three crops the increase was from about 1/4 of production to about 1/2. In all cases the relative decline in the private sector resulted from an absolute decrease in the production eminating from the private sector while at the same time public sector production was increasing. This contrasting experience between the public and private sector was particularly dramatic in the case of grain where private production almost disappeared while in the public sector after a decline in the mid-1960's, production recovered to levels greater than recorded at the beginning of the period.

In general, then, the relatively stagnant performance of Cuban agriculture masks differing trends by sector. On one hand the private sector did very poorly. On the other hand the public sector held its own, as it did in the case of sugar, which registered relatively impressive gains. Indeed if the output trends from private farms had paralleled those which were experienced in the public sector, the agricultural performance in Cuba would have been impressive. Even so, however, Arthur MacEwan a sympathetic critic of the Cuban Revolution, does not even consider Cuba's agricultural public sector experience satisfactory much less what occurred in the private sector. Of sugar, almost entirely a public sector crop, he writes that the "difficulties of sugar production that have continued through the 1970's are a serious weakness in the Cuban economy."[5] Thus, neither sector receives a clean bill of health calling for an analysis of each in turn. We first address the public sector in agriculture and then examine the private sector.

PUBLIC SECTOR

MacEwan's critique of the agricultural public sector heavily emphasizes two internal weaknesses. First, throughout the 1960's the industry experienced an increasingly difficult problem of worker absenteeism and a decline in the intensity of effort by the work force. Second, despite significantly high levels of investment, sugar still by the 1970's was not fully mechanized and levels of productivity remained low. MacEwan finds the source of both of these failures in the organizational structure of the industry. There was, he argues "a failure to organize activities effectively in the mills, in the fields and in transporting canes from fields to mills."[6]

In the pre-revolutionary period intensity of effort was secured from workers through the sanctions of the market. An unsatisfactory work performance or absenteeism could mean that a worker would be removed from employment by a profit-seeking manager. With the Revolution that mechanism was foreclosed. Instead and in place of the market the Cubans attempted to achieve a high level of work effort by tapping the workers' commitment to the Revolution itself. But as several authors have emphasized, such a commitment can easily be dissipated if care is not taken continuously to restrengthen the workers' identification with the Revolution. Efforts to replace this commitment to and willingness to work for the common good appear either not to have occurred sufficiently or else such efforts were not successful enough to produce the required work effort.[7] During the late 1960's problems of disorganization and absenteeism began to become a serious problem, difficulties which MacEwan traces to the failure to develop "any major effort, other than the use of military forms, directed toward the development of organizational structures that might substitute for the traditional coordinating and incentive roles of the market."[8]

One organizational form which might have been of use in addressing these problems was the producer cooperative. The latter is an institution which retains proprietory interests and in that way tends to ensure that a strong work motivation will be present. At the same time the capital/labor wage relationship is avoided since members of the cooperative share its profits. To be sure cooperatives do not represent a structure which encourages work because of commitment to the Revolution. Material incentives are very much a part of the source of its effectiveness. Similarly, with cooperatives, some degree of income inequality seems inevitable. More efficient cooperatives or cooperatives favored by nature or chance will be more profitable than cooperatives which are less efficient or lucky. Thus with cooperatives the work/income association is retained even though it is not expressed as it is in capitalism through a formal labor market.

As we have seen, as written the first agrarian reform called for the creating of cooperatives on expropriated land holdings. But in fact at no time were the sugar estates which were taken over operated as cooperatives. From the beginning they functioned on a wage labor basis rather than having incomes determined by the sharing of profits. The reason the cooperative form was rejected despite its being part of the original agrarian reform law is not entirely clear. Three factors seem however, to have been of importance. Apparently the Cuban leadership was concerned that sugar estate laborers did not possess adequate managerial skills to operate collectives efficiently. This perception of incompetence was traced to the fact that under the old regime their work experience had been confined to wage laborers and not to the administration of their own farms. Second the Government objected to the degree of income inequality which was associated with cooperatives. Finally, there was in Cuba in the early 1960's an ideological predisposition to collective as opposed to individual or cooperative ownership. As Cuba increasingly identified itself as a socialist country the attractiveness of state farms grew since that organizational form was viewed as embodying truely socialist relations of production. In combination these three considerations tended to produce an initial bias toward the model advocated by Thomas in which the public sector is seen as holding pride of place in the countryside.

The hostility towards cooperatives shown by the Cuban Revolution, however, ran contrary to the advice offered by several consultants in the early days of the Revolution, among whom the most important was Rene Dumont. Writing in 1969 Dumont opined that "I continue to believe that [the] refusal to establish agricultural production cooperatives on the expropriated land was a vast mistake." He cites the existence of such cooperatives in other socialist countries as representing a reasonable precedent for the Cubans to have followed, adding derisively "but Cuba wants to be more socialist than the other socialist countries. . . ."[9]

Dumont does concede that if cooperatives had been established they "would naturally have groped about for some time and it would have been necessary to help them get organized," a concession which seems to stem from the argument concerning the workers' lack of experience in managerial roles. But he goes on to assert that by encouraging cooperatives "Cuba would-have *trusted* its agricultural workers, given them more and more responsibilities and they would thus little by little have taken a larger part in the management of their units. . . ." He concludes by arguing that "unless increasing trust is accorded workers, there will be no real progress toward a socialism based on freedom."[10]

Dumont's affirmation of the desirability of cooperatives in socialism ran directly counter to the views of the Cuban leadership. As late as the Party Congress held in 1975 it still was maintained that state farms represented a "superior form of production because it represents ownership by all the people. . . ."[11] Thus whatever merit Dumont's position might possess with regard to increasing agricultural productivity, it is clear that at least through the mid 1970's his ideological position was at sharp variance with those of the Cuban leaders. It was this conflict of views which ensured that Dumont's proposals with regard to cooperatives would be rejected.

Dumont is not the first nor the only one to argue the complementary relationship between cooperatives and socialism. Indeed debate concerning this very subject was especially intense in the Soviet Union during the mid and late 1920's. It was Nikolai Bukharin who argued that the cause of socialism could be advanced by promoting rural cooperatives. Not only, he argued, could the interests of the peasants be served through these institutions but they would also provide the means by which the government could introduce socialism into the countryside on a voluntary basis. His argument was that in a socialist society producer or consumer cooperatives would have to rely for their financing, sources of supply and market outlets on socialist industries and banks. In Bukharin's words they would "become part and parcel of the proletarian economic body." He wrote "the cooperatives will grow into the system of our institutions just as in capitalist society they grow into the system of capitalist relations."[12]

According to Bukharin's biographer, Stephen F. Cohen, few Bolsheviks doubted that cooperatives could be made attractive to the peasants.[13] In effect they were conceeding that a voluntary means by which to overcome the problems associated with small scale agricultural production was readily at hand. But Bukharin's advise was rejected, as was Dumont's in Cuba, because among the Bolsheviks there was wide-spread skepticism that a system of cooperatives would "grow into socialism." The Bolsheviks, like the Cubans of the 1960's and 1970's, believed both that the cooperatives themselves did not embody socialist relations of production and furthermore could not effectively be used to introduce such productive relations. Thus the debate which occurred in Cuba over cooperatives had occurred in the Soviet Union forty years earlier and with the same result.

Thus by the end of the 1970's the Cubans still had not solved the problem of how to organize the public sector in agriculture. The harshness of the labor market was ruled out, but so were cooperatives. At the same time Yugoslov style self-management had not been introduced into the countryside. But this failure to develop new organizational forms was not costless. It meant that production and productivity suffered as workers were not confronted either with the old or a new work incentive system. In all, it is clear that the public sector in Cuban agriculture awaits new departures in organizational structure before sustained increases in efficiency and therefore output can be attained.

PRIVATE SECTOR

Where a private agricultural sector is present its potential contribution to the development effort requires that both adequate incentives be present and that sufficient resources be available to facilitate production. With regard to the first, obviously price levels are a critical variable. They must be sufficiently high to cover costs, including profits, and the latter must be high enough to compensate for either foregone leisure or the opportunity costs associated with possible alternative employment opportunities. Furthermore an adequate supply of consumer goods must be available to allow farmers to turn their extra income into the possession of real goods and services. Second, even in the context of a highly motivated peasantry technical and financial assistance must be made available to the farmers in order for them to increase their productive capacity. One form this might take is subsidized credit directed to the agricultural community in order to encourage the purchase of new tools and equipment. Another form this might take is the providing of an effective technical extension service in order to acquaint farmers with relevant productivity-raising methods of production. Finally, if the small size of the producing unit, in the context of peasant farming, does constrain productivity some form of voluntary association among the farmers must be encouraged. These associations, whether they are formally cooperatives or not, are important in order to enable these producers to transcend the constraints associated with small farms. With them capital equipment might be more efficiently employed. Similarly with such voluntary associations technical advances which might be passed over in small-scale ventures might be introduced.

To state these conditions for successful private sector agriculture is to suggest how poorly, on an ideological level, the Cuban Revolution was equipped to promote expansion in this sector. As we have seen throughout the 1960's it opposed the use of material incentives as a way of stimulating production. Furthermore it was not enthusiastic about cooperatives. Under these circumstances an accomodation with the proprietory interests of Cuba's farmers was unlikely. Similarly it was unlikely that the peasant sector, seen by the head of Cuba's Agrarian Reform Institute Carlos Rafael Rodriguez as "an island in a Socialist ocean" would have sufficient resources diverted to it to raise its level of technology and efficiency. The public sector was viewed as the preferred sector and the peasantry treated as a backwater. This essentially hostile view of the private sector is captured in a statement concerning the peasantry by Rodriguez himself:

> by fixing just prices for the produce of the small peasant the Cuban revolution is far from being guided by the 'get rich' slogan of Bukharin addressed to the Kulak. These are purchasing prices which would stimulate the most efficient farming methods but do not result in either excessive accumulation or indolence. More, the

> peasant cannot use his income to acquire machines, for their sale to private individuals is prohibited, or more land, since the state has the priority to buy land put up for sale and moreover can forbid sales, making for excessive individual holdings.[14]

From this statement it is clear that mistrust of the private sector meant that the Cubans were following policies whose effect was to constrain the productive capability of this sector.

The Cuban leadership thus was reluctant to satisfy any of the conditions essential if the private sector were effectively to contribute to the country's development effort. Under these conditions the stagnation of output which we observed from the private sector is entirely predictable and understandable. It reflected the profound ambivalence which the Cuban Revolution possessed with regard to the small farm community. On one hand its own agrarian reform law perpetuated and augmented this sector. But on the other hand its policies were designed to limit the dynamism which such a sector could potentially release. In short the Government's ideology was responsible for the policies which resulted in the private sector's unsatisfactory production trends. Obviously such ambivalence comes at a high price for a country like Cuba which is attempting to attain self-reliant growth. By eliminating the potential for economic advance from one-third of the agricultural sector the Cuban leadership inflicted on itself a serious handicap to its attaining its own economic goals.

There is some recent evidence suggesting that the Cuban leadership has begun to rethink its perverse policies with regard to the private sector. This reevaluation is especially centered on the role of cooperatives in the private sector and to some extent also on the incentive system which should be used to encourage production. In May of 1977 the National Association of Small Farmers (ANAP) under the direction of the Cuban Communist Party, began to encourage the formation of cooperatives among peasant farmers. From an insigificant 43 in 1975 the number of such cooperatives increase to 363 in 1978 and 1017 by September 1980.[15] According to one source the cooperatives have become "the apple of the state's eye."[16]

Fidel Castro himself suggested the magnitude of the rethinking which has gone on in his address to the Second Congress of the Communist Party of Cuba in December 1980. There he declared that "the achievements scored by the cooperatives in the socio-economic and political fields open up excellent prospects for this higher form of production." He goes on to say that "our Revolution should have promoted cooperatives earlier." He further reports that the economic benefits of cooperatives are already in evidence: "in general, cooperatives have high yields – twice or even three times as much as the individual lots that were incorporated in the cooperatives – thanks to the introduction of mechanization and technology."[17]

What is most significant in Castro's address is his statement, for the first time, that cooperatives represented a "higher form of production." What this means is that they are not now considered to be bourgeois institutions and are not to be considered inconsistent with the socialist goals of the Cuban Revolution. The full line of reasoning which lies behind this new analysis was not made clear in Castro's address. It is likely, however, that in ways perhaps not so different from those argued by Bukharin the Cuban leadership now views cooperatives as the means by which better to integrate the peasantry in its Revolution. Castro concluded his discussion of cooperatives by declaring that cooperatives "now with the full backing of the Party and the state . . . will make up for lost time."[18]

A similarly but perhaps less through-going change in attitude has occurred with regard to the use of prices as an incentive mechanism to stimulate agricultural production. In mid-1980 the Government, for the first time, allowed peasants who had met their delivery quotas to state agencies to market their surpluses on free markets. It is far too early to determine the full significance of this new policy. However, the general impression which is gained is that this new departure, like that with regard to cooperatives, has been successful in stimulating production. Recent visitors to Cuba report that as a result of the use of the market there has been "a substantial rise in agricultural output and an easing of urban food shortages."[19] At the same time there is concern about the relatively high prices which prevail in the *mercados libre*.

On this subject Fidel Castro is considerably less effusive than he is on the question of cooperatives. In the course of his report to the Party Congress he merely mentions that "the farm market for unrationed produce has begun operating this year,"[20] with none of the enthusiastic discussion which accompanied his analysis of producer cooperatives in agriculture. Free markets, like cooperatives, clearly have the potential for stimulating production. But at least until now the undisguised appeal to material incentives, which the resort to the market implies, still does not sit well with the Cuban leadership.

The issue which suggests itself in this context is the extent to which, in their reversal concerning cooperatives and markets, the Cuban leadership has at last confronted the policy constraints implied by the existence of a private sector in agriculture. In attempting to stimulate production by using cooperatives and markets they give evidence that they are now willing to accept a greater degree of rural income inequality than they once might have so long as greater production is the result. In the past these institutions were considered unacceptable, at least in part because of the effect they would have on rural income differentiation. As a consequence, production stagnated. It may be that the leadership has now adjusted its priorities and in its search for increased output will tolerate a greater degree of inequality than it did in the past.

So far, institutional reform in agriculture has been confined to the private sector. No comparable announcements of changes in approach have been made with regard to state farms. But it is hard to believe that if cooperatives are effective in stimulating productivity among small farmers that the Cubans will not be tempted to extend this organizational form into the public sector as well. Of course circumstances in the two sphere are not identical. In particular the old objection that sugar workers have never filled a proprietory function and will not be able effectively to participate in the management of a cooperative venture will be raised. But it is at least possible that this objection and the problems which stem from it may pale relative to the urgency of increasing production. If so, it is entirely possible that during the 1980's there may be some experimentation with the introduction of cooperative farms in the public sector as well as in the private sector and at least a limited use of material incentives as a means of increasing worker output among wage earners in agriculture.

The Cuban experience, then, suggests that it may not be necessary to choose between Beckford's and Thomas' approach to land reform. It is possible to create an agricultural structure part of which is composed of peasants and part of which represents public sector agriculture. But at the same time, Cuba's revolution demonstrates that land reform alone, of whatever kind, is not sufficient to ensure expanding output. Policies must be implemented and institutions must be created which will result in both an intense work effort and efficient use of resources. In the Cuban case at least it is this post-land reform phase of policy-making in which failings have been most marked. In particular it is clear that there was a conflict between the Revolutionary leadership's desire to create what it considered socialist relations of production and what was necessary to achieve an expansion in the capacity to produce agricultural goods.

The Cuban agricultural reform history then is of relevance to the rest of the Caribbean. What appears as a stark choice between two competing models of agrarian reform – a peasantry or state farms – may not in fact represent a profound dilemma. But at the same time, the need to match policy with the requirements of growth looms as a possible difficulty, all the more so if ideological constraints on policy are important. Growth in agriculture involves motivating farmers and equipping them with the means to expand output. Especially the first – finding and effective and acceptable system of work motivation – may turn out to be the critical issue upon which success is stimulating agricultural modernization in autonomous growth hinges.

NOTES

1. Arthur MacEwan, "Cuban Agriculture and Development: Contradictions and Progress," in Dharam Ghai, Azizur Rahman Khan, Eddy Lee and Samir Radwan (Eds.) *Agrarian Systems and Rural Development* (New York: Holmes and Meier Publisher, Inc., 1979), p. 339.
2. Arthur MacEwan, *Revolution and Economic Development in Cuba* (New York: St. Martin's Press, 1981), p. 73.
3. Arthur MacEwan, *Revolution and Economic Development in Cuba* (New York: St. Martin's Press, 1981), p. 73.
4. Arthur MacEwan, "Cuban Agriculture and Development," p. 335.
5. Arthur MacEwan, *Revolution and Economic Development in Cuba*, p. 191.
6. *Ibid.*, p. 194.

7. Bertram Silverman, "The Great Debate in Retrospect: Economic Rationality and the Ethics of Revolution," in Bertram Silverman (Ed.) *Man and Socialism in Cuba* The Great Debate (New York: Atreneum, 1971), p. 23; Robert M. Bernardo. *The Theory of Moral Incentives in Cuba* (University of Alabama Press, 1971).
8. Arthur MacEwan, *Revolution and Economic Development in Cuba*, p. 148.
9. Rene Dumont. *Cuba: Socialism and Development* (New York: Grove Press, Inc., 1970), p. 229.
10. Rene Dumont, *Cuba: Socialism and Development*, p. 230; emphasis in original.
11. Arthur MacEwan, *Revolution and Economic Development in Cuba*, p. 207. This quotation represents MacEwan's paraphrasing of *Theses and Resolutions Concerning the Agrarian Question and the Relations with the Peasantry* written at the First Congress of the Communist Party of Cuba.
12. Stephan F. Cohen, *Bukharin and the Bolshevik Revolution*, A Political Biography 1888–1938 (New York: Afred A. Knopf, 1973), 195–6.
13. Stephan F. Cohen, *Bukharin and the Bolshevik Revolution*, p. 197–198.
14. Quoted in Arthur MacEwan, *Revolution and Economic Development in Cuba*, p. 89.
15. Fidel Castro, "Main Report to Second Congress of Communist Party of Cuba" *Cuba Update*, Vol. II, No. 1, March 1981, p. 22.
16. Latin America Regional Reports, *Caribbean* 8 May, 1981, p. 3.
17. Fidel Castro, "Main Report to the Second Congress of the Communist Party of Cuba", p. 22.
18. Fidel Castro, "Main Report to the Second Congress of the Communist Party of Cuba", p. 22.
19. Maxine Molyneux and Fred Halliday, "Austerity with a Human Face," *In These Times*, June 3–16, 1981, p. 13.
20. Fidel Castro, "Main Report to the Second Congress of the Communist Party of Cuba", p. 7.

Chapter 8

The Strike of Capital in Jamaica

Guyana and Jamaica were the "Left" governments in the English-speaking Caribbean during the 1970's. But data from that decade indicate that neither country was successful in its efforts at initiating autonomous growth. In both countries per capita economic growth rates were negative between 1970 and 1977. In the case of Jamaica the 1.7 percent annual rate of decline in per capita output reversed a pattern of expansion which in the 1960s exceeded 2.0 percent per year. Similarly the decrease of 0.7 percent per year in Guyana reversed a pattern of expansion which had been experienced in all but the riot torn years of the 1960s. (See Table 8.1.)

Equally significant are the data provided in Table 8.2 on agricultural output in these countries. There it is made clear that the shift to a strategy of autonomous growth in these countries was not accompanied by a new dynamic in agricultural output. In both Jamaica and Guyana agricultural output per

Table 8.1

AVERAGE ANNUAL GROWTH RATE OF REAL GROSS DOMESTIC PRODUCT PER CAPITA GUYANA AND JAMAICA, 1950/60–1970/77

	1950–60	1960–65	1965–70	1970–77
Guyana	1.4	–0.8	1.5	–0.7
Jamaica	6.5	2.1	3.9	–1.7

Revised and calculated from the source: International Bank for Reconstruction and Development, *World Tables*, 2nd ed., 1980 (Baltimore and London: The Johns Hopkins University Press, 1980), p. 374.

Table 8.2

AVERAGE ANNUAL GROWTH RATE OF AGRICULTURAL PRODUCTION PER CAPITA GUYANA AND JAMAICA 1950/60–1970/77

	1950–60	1960–65	1965–70	1970–77
Guyana	-	−2.9	−1.1	−0.3
Jamaica	1.4	1.6	−2.5	−2.8

Revised and calculated from the source: Calculated from "Comparative Economic Data," Table 1, in International Bank for Reconstruction and Development, *World Tables*, 2nd ed., 1980 (Baltimore and London: The Johns Hopkins University Press, 1980).

capita actually declined in the 1970s. In Guyana this decrease continued a trend traceable at least to the early 1960s, while in Jamaica that negative performance seems to have been initiated in the late 1960s. In both cases, therefore, the shift to self-reliant growth was not accompanied by a reversal of previous unsatisfactory performances in agriculture despite the fact that the new approach to development required such as reversal.

In this chapter we analyze Jamaica's experience under the Michael Manley government and democratic socialism. In this effort we seek to account for the poor economic performance which characterized Jamaica in the 1970s. In the chapter which follows we do the same for the Guyanese case.

The Jamaica in which Michael Manley and the People's National Party came to office in 1972 was a much more economically advanced country than Guyana. Not only was its per capita output higher and its recent growth rates more rapid, but it had been the recipient of far more foreign investment. The mining of bauxite, tourism and light manufacturing were all important and expanding sectors of economic activity, and all were dependent upon foreign sources of investment as well as market outlets. Direct foreign investment in 1971 in Jamaica, for example, amounted to $176.0 million (US), a level which ranked Jamaica among the leading countries in the world on a per capita basis.[1] Yet, as we have seen, the prosperity which Jamaica had experienced had not alleviated the extensive social problems of the country and poverty and unemployment persisted at high levels.

Michael Manley's 1972 cabinet has been described as "liberal, middle class, technocratic and sophisticated . . . steeped in the social welfare traditions of activist government."[2] As such it immediately set to work to develop programs to address Jamaica's problems. The first two years of the PNP government saw initiatives in many directions. It moved to create employment opportunities through the establishment of public works programs; it established minimum wage legislation; it initiated a subsidized housing program and engaged in an extensive adult literacy campaign. In addition, for the first time, tuition charges for secondary and university education were eliminated and a substantial reduction in lunch costs at schools was put in place. Finally, charges were reduced or eliminated at the country's public health clinics and hospitals.

In addition to these domestic initiatives the Manley government also took steps to change the long-standing relationship which existed between the Jamaican government and the foreign-owned bauxite industry. The latter through the 1960s had been a principal source of the economic growth which had been experienced in the country. But the contribution which it made to the well-being of the country was limited in two ways. First, it was virtually an enclave industry. It engaged in only limited processing of the bauxite in Jamaica itself. Aside from labor, it purchased very little from the local economy and therefore only minimally stimulated other separate but related activities. Taxes, secondly, therefore were the only other means by which the industry could contribute to the Jamaican economy. But as Norman Girvan has argued "because of the peculiar problem of taxing a commodity which is not sold, but merely transferred between branches of the same company, the industry has been considerably under-taxed."[3]

It was to correct this latter problem that the Manley government moved in 1974. In that year the government initiated negotiations with the six North American aluminum companies operating in Jamaica to change the contracts under which they operated in the country. Two goals motivated the government's initiative. First, following Girvan's analysis, it wanted to increase the level of revenue received by the government from the bauxite operations. Second, it wished to establish a governmental equity share in the industry. Presumably the intention was to gain a voice in managerial decisions in the industry and in this way increase the stimulus which the industry contributed to the whole Jamaican economy.

The bauxite companies flatly refused to negotiate with the government. In response, the Manley government passed a bauxite production levy. With this new legislation the level of taxation was indexed to the price of aluminum ingot sold in the United States. In so doing the government circumvented the problem of ascertaining the true price of the bauxite when it was sold from one subsidiary of the parent firm to another. In addition, the legislation contained a provision establishing minimal levels of taxation thus discouraging companies from reducing output to reduce their tax liability. Generally the levy worked as anticipated and substantially increased the revenue the government received from the industry. Indeed, Runsford W. Palmer has written that

> the Jamaican bauxite levy . . . must rank as one of the finer strategies by a developing country to increase its share of the gains from commerical exploitation of its natural resources while at the same time insulating its revenues against inflation abroad.[4]

With the passage of the levy, negotiations were initiated and resulted in the government's securing a 51 percent equity share in the industry. It also vested in itself ownership rights to the lands controlled by the bauxite company, but not ownership of the bauxite itself. In this regard, however, it does not appear that the government was successful in substantially influencing managerial decisions. The enclave nature of the industry remained intact. Indeed, this failure was anticipated by C. Y. Thomas in 1974 when he wrote that even government ownership of 51 percent of a local subsidiary does not substantially diminish the power of foreign firms in managerial decisions and as a result is "not capable of yielding any significant changes in the structure of production relations."[5] In sum as a result of its negotiations with the industry the Manley government was able to increase the tax yield derived from the industry, but did not achieve a decisive voice in production decisions.

It was in the context of its negotiations with the bauxite companies that the Manley government announced its commitment to democratic socialism. Motivation for the timing of this declaration is not completely clear. One hypothesis is that it was intended to demonstrate the government's seriousness of purpose in the negotiations and in that way increase its bargaining leverage with the bauxite companies. Another view, not necessarily inconsistent with the first, is that after two years in office the Manley government had concluded that in the face of domestic and overseas opposition, if it were to achieve its goals "it would have to mobilize as much support as possible" and that "the democratic socialism campaign was the perfect way to build that support."[6] The Prime Minister himself wrote in defense of the program that there was "no doubt about the need for fundamental change" but "there was an urgent need to educate the nation to a more complete understanding of what the processes of change would demand of the people." To do this there had to be "a re-examination of our basic philosophy in the light of the present circumstances in Jamaica and the outside world."[7] Read carefully this statement is consistent with either or both of the two hypotheses suggested above. It is therefore likely that the democratic socialism campaign represented an effort to mobilize political support at least in part as a way of influencing the bauxite negotiations.

Whatever the explanation of the timing of democratic socialism it is quite clear that, in its intent as compared to its effect, the campaign was not envisioned as a sharp break with the social democratic and liberal politics of the preceding two years. In identifying countries with which it shared "socialist" convictions, the Manley government named Sweden, Holland, Britain, New Zealand, Tanzania, Australia, Zambia and India. Pointedly omitted from this list were Cuba, a country with whom Jamaica had recently established diplomatic relations, China or any COMECON country.

The democratic socialism program did not envision nationalization, expropriation or a substantial change in economic ownership. Despite the fact that Manley declared that "the days of capitalism are over. . . . Socialism is running the country now" he also acknowledged that "private enterprise and economic activity can be a most effective way of producing the general run of services in a country."[8] The PNP pamphlet on democratic socialism specifically noted that private foreign capital remained welcome in Jamaica.[9]

Despite this intended continuity, the 1974 ideological offensive was very exciting and tended to take on a life of its own. Government-sponsored rallies were well attended throughout the country. The campaign seems to have unleashed a deeply felt hope that, at last, present in Jamaica was a government committed to the elevation of the living standards and dignity of the population. In short, the democratic socialism program encouraged the hope and started to create the belief that in the future, unlike the past, economic growth could be harnessed to satisfy the basic needs of the Jamaican people.

But of course associated with such an ideological campaign are profound risks. Especially these risks are strong in a country as dependent on foreign investment for its economic growth as Jamaica had been. For, sources of investment capital abroad possess the power to undermine that growth simply by deciding not to invest in the country. Precisely such a decision becomes more likely when, for example, the adoption of a new ideology threatens to upset the stability of the receiving country. It is not easy to discern at what point such a "strike of capital" might occur. Many variables enter into the business decision concerning investment. The presumption is that so long as an investment project remains suitably profitable capital inflows will continue. But profits can only be anticipated, not guaranteed, at the time that the decision to invest is made. As a result, a subjective assessment of circumstances must inevitably occur. A socialist ideological offensive, no matter how moderate in actual content, runs the risk of creating sufficient uncertainty that there will be reduction in the flow of foreign investment.

Data on foreign investment as seen in Table 8.3 suggest that there was just such a reaction to the democratic socialist campaign. Overseas private investment in Jamaica peaked in 1971 at about $176.0 million (US). It declined in the next two years, but even so stood at $75.1 million in 1973. In 1974, however, the year of the campaign, the bottom fell out of the inflow of

Table 8.3

NET DIRECT FOREIGN INVESTMENT IN JAMAICA, 1970–78
(millions of US dollars)

Year	Investment
1970	$161.4
1971	176.0
1972	97.8
1973	75.1
1974	23.3
1975	–1.8
1976	–0.6
1977	–7.0
1978	–24.0*

Revised and calculated from the source: International Bank of Reconstruction and Development, *World Tables*, 2nd ed., 1980, p. 314.

* 1978 provided by Bank of Jamaica.

capital, declining by 69 percent to $23.3 million. By 1975 new foreign investment completely dried up. Jamaica for the years from 1975 through 1978 was a net exporter of capital rather than a recipient. In effect foreign capital simply refused to come to Jamaica any longer.

The drying up of foreign investment had its counterpart in production itself. In both manufacturing and mining, the two sectors of the economy most heavily dependent on investment from abroad, previous upward trends in production reversed. In both cases the value of output peaked in 1974 and thereafter declined. In mining the contribution to Jamaica's gross domestic product declined by 28 percent between 1974 and 1977 and in the case of manufacturing the fall was 8.8 percent (see Table 8.4).

The thesis suggested here that these decreases represented a reaction against democratic socialism has been denied by the West Indian economist, Compton Bourne. Bourne writes that

Table 8.4
CONTRIBUTION TO JAMAICAN GROSS DOMESTIC PRODUCT BY INDUSTRIAL ORIGIN, 1970–1977
(millions in 1974 Jamaican dollars)

Year	Agriculture	Mining	Manufacturing
1970	149.8	199.8	344.4
1971	167.6	215.9	351.9
1972	170.7	232.1	384.9
1973	159.4	261.9	379.9
1974	162.7	297.3	386.5
1975	164.9	227.6	385.8
1976	166.3	183.3	373.0
1977	176.6	214.5	352.6

Revised and calculated from the source: International Bank for Reconstruction and Development, *World Tables*, 2nd ed., 1980, pp. 114–115.

> while it is tempting to attempt to explain the recent investment performance in terms of a capital strike by foreign and local firms in response to the democratic socialist posture of the Jamaican government, more plausible economic reasons can be identified.

The reasons cited by Bourne are first, a profit squeeze caused by rising input costs in the face of domestic price rigidities. In turn these were at least in part caused by government price controls and the increase in the government's debt which occurred in this period. Bourne's argument is that a decrease in profits "resulted in lower levels of domestic resource accumulation" while the "main effect" of increased government spending and borrowing was "the substitution of public consumption and less productive expenditure for more productive private expenditures." He goes on to assert that "bureaucratic growth, through its resource allocative effect . . . undermined the productive capacity and performance of the economy . . ."[10] In effect Compton Bourne's argument is that the decrease in investment and production which occurred was not a strike by capital but a rational response to changed economic conditions, only marginally related to the government's ideological offensive.

Bourne's arguments in support of this position are not at all convincing. For example, the data which he presents with regard to the adequacy of profits are not strong enough to support the burden which he places upon them. Table 8.5 reproduces the information which Bourne presents with regard

Table 8.5

PROFITS IN THE JAMAICAN ECONOMY, 1970–77

Year	Millions of Jamaican Dollars	As Percentage of Gross National Product
1970–73	$370	31%
1974	411	34
1977	334	30

Revised and calculated from the source: Compton Bourne, "Jamaica and the International Monetary Fund: Economics of the 1978 Stabilization Program," *Studies in Rural Finance* (Agricultural Finance Program, The Ohio State University, 1980), p. 14.

to profits in the Jamaican economy. It is surprising to note, in light of his position, that profits actually rose in 1974 both absolutely and as a percentage of the national income. It was that year in which investment dropped precipitously. Clearly this decline cannot be accounted for by the profits performance since 1974 was not a bad year when viewed from a narrow economic point of view.

In the years thereafter profits did fall, but it is also striking that as a share of the national income they tended to hold their own, declining only from an average of 31 percent in 1970–73 to 30 percent in 1977. In light of these data it does not seem warranted to talk of a "profits depression" as Bourne does.[11] It is particularly questionable whether the kind of decreases revealed here, taken alone and without reference to the government's new ideology, can account for the precipitous decreases in investment which occurred in Jamaica in these years.

The fact that investment declined so markedly despite the fact that profits tended to hold their own casts doubt on Bourne's second argument that government's borrowing diverted resources from productive to unproductive uses. In this regard Bourne's employs a "crowding out" thesis in which it is asserted that the public sector's need to finance its debt displaced private sector borrowing. As he puts it "through its credit and fiscal operations, the Jamaican government succeeded in bidding away real resources on an increasing scale."[12] But Bourne omits an absolutely critical element in presenting this argument. What is required in presenting the crowding out thesis is a specification of the hypothetical alternative. It must at least be argued that the private sector would have, in the absence of the government, bid for the credit which in fact went to the public sector. Only if it can plausibly be argued that the private sector would have been active in the money market can it be argued that the government's participation in that market acted to crowd out the business firms. If this cannot be argued persuasively the government's activities cannot be said to represent a diversion of resources. Indeed in such circumstances government's borrowing was a stimulative prop to an otherwise depressed economy.

In fact there are grave questions which can be raised concerning the thesis that credit unavailability is what caused the decrease in investment in Jamaica in the 1970s. For it was foreign investment which experienced the earliest and ultimately most dramatic decreases. In 1975 when foreign investment had already completely dried up, domestic investment levels were still increasing. Even in 1976 investment from local sources still approximated the 1972 levels. It was not until 1977, the third straight year that foreign investment in the country was negative, that local investment fell to very low levels. (See Table 8.6).

What is significant about this is that it must be assumed that it is the local investors who are the more sensitive to local credit market conditions than foreign businesses. Multinational corporations by definition are not constrained to Jamaican sources of credit if they desire financing. Thus the investment decline was experienced most dramatically in the sector which was most protected from crowding out and occurred least in the

Table 8.6

INVESTMENT SOURCES IN THE JAMAICAN ECONOMY, 1972–77

Year	Gross Domestic Investment	Direct Foreign Investment	Investment from Local Sources
1972	$521.6	$97.8	$423.8
1973	606.3	75.1	531.2
1974	539.7	23.3	516.4
1975	554.5	–1.8	556.3
1976	415.9	–0.6	416.5
1977	265.7	–7.0	272.7

Revised and calculated from the source: International Bank for Reconstruction and Development, *World Tables*, 2nd ed., 1980, pp. 314, 380.

sector where crowding out could have been expected to have its most important impact. At least until 1977, several years after the Jamaican economy had gone into decline, the crowding out thesis does not seem to fit the nation's experience.

What clearly is suggested in all of this is that conditions in Jamaica's money markets were not dominant in dictating the level of investment which was undertaken. Even if more credit had been available it is likely that this would not have had much of an impact on investors – especially those from abroad. If this is so then even at reduced levels of public borrowing investment in the Jamaican economy would have been depressed.

If by a "strike of capital" it is meant a decrease in investment caused by a "noneconomic" change in the investment climate then this seems to have been what Jamaica experienced. Seen from the point of view of foreign firms, the articulation of democratic socialism introduced new elements of risk and uncertainty. This, in conjunction with stable current profits, seems to have been sufficient to dissuade foreign management from making new commitments to the country. As a result investment fell literally to nothing, a situation which was disastrous for a country like Jamaica where previous development had centered on foreign investment.

Almost overnight, therefore, Jamaica was thrown onto its own resources if growth were to continue. But it is quite clear that the Manley government was not prepared for the strike of foreign capital which had occurred and was not ready to institute new policies for growth based on domestic resources. This lack of preparedness can be seen in two ways. First, the PNP government in articulating its philosophy of democratic socialism had anticipated a continued inflow of foreign capital. It had announced that "foreign private capital is welcome in Jamaica and is assured of fair and consistent treatment."[13] Second, it is now clear that the government had not prepared contingency plans to be implemented if a strike of capital were to occur. In particular, the Manley government had not worked out a means to mobilize the countryside in order to tap investible resources, a strategy which, as we have seen, is essential if autonomous growth is to be successful. When foreign investment came to a halt, this failure to develop plans for self-reliant growth meant that the Jamaican economy fell into a catastrophic depression.

The Manley government's program for agriculture was far less extensive than what was required under the circumstances. It contained two principal components. On one hand it encouraged the *establishing* of cooperatives in the sugar industry. On the other hand it initiated a land reform program under the name "Land Lease." But it is quite clear that even if these programs had been successful in their own terms, their scope was far less than what had been envisioned by either C. Y. Thomas or George Beckford or what would have been required to allow the country to develop on its own. Thus the cooperative program was confined to the reorganization of the only three sugar estates which were publicly owned.[14] The Land Lease program involved leasing of land in small plots and the provision of credit to the individual renters. However the number of farmers who were able to participate in the program was severely constrained since, as in the case of sugar cooperatives, the only lands included in the program were those already owned by the government. As a result, in the absence of extensive land purchases by the government, neither of these programs could substantially alter the basic structure of Jamaica's agriculture.

It is not surprising, therefore, that Tables 8.7 and 8.8 which report on agriculture's performance during the years of the PNP government do not show the kind of expansion which was necessary for autonomous growth to be achieved. From the point of view of physical output the country's principal crops all experienced substantial decreases during the 1970s. The output of sugar and coffee in 1978 was only about three-fourths the level achieved in 1970, while in the case of bananas production came to only about three-fifths of the 1970 level. Only in the case of cocoa did production increase, but even so the 1978 level of output just approximated the production achieved in 1965. A similar pattern of stagnation is told in terms of the value of output for agriculture as a whole. It was not until 1977

Table 8.7

INDEX OF PHYSICAL PRODUCTION: JAMAICA, 1965–78
1970 = 100

Year	Sugar	Bananas	Coffee	Cocoa
1965	132	112	81	152
1966	135	124	66	103
1967	121	141	68	41
1968	120	114	75	98
1969	103	112	56	97
1970	100	100	100	100
1971	102	94	98	87
1972	101	95	82	135
1973	88	80	56	27
1974	99	53	17	78
1975	96	52	27	97
1976	98	59	4	94
1977	89	60	125	108
1978	77	58	72	155

Revised and calculated from the source: Compton Bourne, "Jamaica and the International Monetary Fund: Economics of the 1978 Stabilization Program," *Studies in Rural Finance* (Agricultural Finance Program, The Ohio State University, 1980), p. 11.

Table 8.8
VALUE OF JAMAICAN AGRICULTURAL OUTPUT, 1970–77
(millions in 1974 Jamaican dollars)

Year	Value
1970	$149.8
1971	107.6
1972	170.7
1973	159.4
1974	162.7
1975	164.9
1976	166.3
1977	176.6

Revised and calculated from the source: International Bank for Reconstruction and Development, *World Tables*, 2nd ed., 1980, pp. 114–115.

that the 1972 market value of agricultural production was attained. In the latter year agriculture's contribution to the gross domestic production was only about 3.5 percent higher than it had been in 1972. Clearly no sustained upward trend in agriculture had occurred. As a result this sector did not offset the deficiencies in the Jamaica economy which resulted from the decline of foreign investment.

It is easy therefore to establish that, as revealed in its agricultural policies, the Manley government's response to the economic crisis was inadequate. The government simply did not have a program which could replace the resources lost as a result of the drying up of foreign investment. But this failure raises a problem, for the Manley government could count among its advisors both George Beckford and Clive Thomas. It was thus unlikely that the arguments concerning the necessity for an extensive agricultural reorganization and modernization program had not at least received a hearing among policymakers. Simple ignorance of what was needed could not therefore be the explanation of the government's weakness in its approach to agriculture.

Rather this failure must be sought in its ideological commitments. It must be remembered that substantively the Manley government never was a radical government intent on a thorough reorganization of Jamaican society. Despite its socialist rhetoric at no time did the government, either in practice or in theory, challenge the legitimacy of the private ownership of industry or agriculture. To be sure the private sector, particularly the foreign-based private sector, reacted very negatively to the rhetoric and reduced its commitments to the country sharply. But this was not what the government had hoped would happen and in fact this reaction severely handicapped it in its effort to carry through its social democratic political agenda. At the same time the kind of agricultural reorganization advocated by Beckford and Thomas is truly a radical, if not revolutionary act. Both advocated a frontal attack on the concentrated land ownership pattern of the country in which private ownership of large scale holdings would be completely eliminated. Quite clearly this kind of change was beyond the limits which the Manley government set for itself. Manley himself attested to his essential political moderation in a remark he made to Andrew Young: "I just happen to be a friend of Castro's. I'm certain that he views me as a fuzzy liberal. I'm a Democratic Socialist and he is a firm Communist, and that is an essential difference."[15] Nelson Keith has made the same point more analytically: "the strategies formulated by the [Manley] Government should not be taken as the initiation of an alternative mode of production but rather as a strategy to mitigate class conflict within on-going capitalist relations."[16]

The government of Michael Manley was unable to cope with a whirlwind which it itself had at least partially set into motion. In its effort to mobilize support for its program of reform it had employed language which proved to be more inflammatory than it intended. A flight of capital was triggered and this caused a severe economic downturn. For this economic decline to have been overcome radical agricultural policies were required, programs well beyond the ideological constraints which the government accepted. As a result it was immobilized: trapped between the negative actions of the foreign investor and its own commitment to political moderation. It was this immobility, of course, which resulted in its loss of power in the election held in October 1980.

NOTES

1. International Bank for Reconstruction and Development, *World Tables*, 2nd ed., 1980, from the data files of the World Bank (Baltimore and London: The Johns Hopkins University Press, 1980), p. 314.
2. The Epica Task Force, *Jamaica: Caribbean Challenge* (Washington: Epica Task Force, 1978), p. 58.
3. Norman Girvan, *Foreign Capital and Economic Underdevelopment in Jamaica* (Jamaica: Institute of Social and Economic Research, University of the West Indies, 1971), p. 261.
4. Ransford W. Palmer, *Caribbean Dependence on the United States Economy* (New York: Praeger Publishers, 1979), p. 118.
5. Clive Y. Thomas, *Dependence and Transformation: The Economics of the Transition to Socialism* (New York: Monthly Review Press, 1974), p. 98.
6. Epica Task Force, *Jamaica: Caribbean Challenge*, p. 68.
7. *Democratic Socialism for Jamaica* (Jamaica: The Agency for Public Information, Government of Jamaica), p. 4.
8. Epica Task Force, *Jamaica: Caribbean Challenge*, p. 68.
9. *Democratic Socialism for Jamaica*, p. 3.
10. Compton Bourne, "Jamaica and the International Monetary Fund: Economics of the 1978 Stabilization Program," *Studies in Rural Finance* (Agricultural Finance Program, The Ohio State University, 1980), pp. 14, 16, 18.
11. Bourne, "Jamaica and the International Monetary Fund," p. 14.
12. Bourne, "Jamaica and the International Monetary Fund," p. 17.
13. *Democratic Socialism for Jamaica*, p. 3.
14. Carl Stone, "An Appraisal of the Co-operative Process in the Jamaican Sugar Industry," *Social and Economic Studies* 27, 1 (March 1978):1.
15. *Washington Post*, August 25, 1980.
16. Nelson Willoughby Keith, *A Development Strategy in Historico-Structural Perspective: Dependence, Dependency Management and the Bauxite Policies in Jamaica* (Unpublished Ph.D. Dissertation, Rutgers University, 1981), p. 25.

Chapter 9

The Post-Colonial Mode of Production in Guyana

In the years immediately after independence in 1966, Guyana, like the other countries of the Caribbean, adopted the development strategy recommended by W. Arthur Lewis. Guyana, however, was poorly equipped to attract investment capital from abroad. The country had been the site of a truely terrifying period of conflict between its major ethnic groups – black descendents of slaves and East Indian descendents of indentured immigrants between 1962 and 1964. The interrelated divisions and tensions which resulted in that communal strife meant that very little investment was made in the country in the late 1960s and early 1970s. Its 1973 Annual Economic Survey summarized its difficulties in this regard quite succinctly: ". . . despite numerous incentives and encouragement in the form of tax holidays and duty free concessions, [manufacturing] remained dormant with very little expansion and diversification."[1] In short, in its first years of independence, Guyana was a nation deadlocked in its effort to achieve economic development.

Under these circumstances and because of increasing domestic political pressure, the government of Prime Minister Forbes Burnham moved sharply to the Left in the 1970s.[2] This process started first in 1972 with the nationalization of the principal firm in the bauxite industry. Acts of nationalization thereafter were carried out in large sections of trade, distribution, transportation, communications, and the remaining firm in bauxite. Finally, in 1976, the government nationalized the economy-dominating sugar industry. By 1977, the government estimated that about 80 percent of the economy rested in the hands of the public sector.

In a major speech in 1974, the Prime Minister declared that Guyana had chosen "socialism" as its instrument of economic development and it was deliberate policy to vest ownership of

Guyanese resources in Guyanese hands.[3] Guyana's socialism, according to official declarations, was not intended to be state dominated. According to the constitution of the ruling party, cooperatives were intended to be "the main instrument of achieving the objectives of the [socialist] ideology."[4] Prime Minister Burnham, in his 1974 speech, asserted that the co-operative should be "the principal institution for giving the masses the control of our economy." It was, he went on to say, the government's "declared objective [to make] the cooperative sector the dominant sector eventually."[5]

As a result the cooperative sector has received extensive government encouragement, most notably the establishment of the Guyana National Cooperative Bank, designed specifically to finance the growth of these institutions. By the end of 1975, despite a relatively small contribution to the output of the economy, the cooperative sector, according to official statistics, had enrolled over 120,000 people in 1,327 cooperative societies.[6]

In addition to these domestic initiatives, Guyana's reputation as a radical state was further reinforced in the 1970s by its foreign policy. Long before the other Caribbean countries followed its lead, Guyana sought out friendly relations with the government of Fidel Castro. Furthermore, it actively supported the guerilla forces of the M.P.L.A. in Angola by permitting planes carrying Cuban troops to Africa to refuel at Timehri International Airport. In both of these actions, Guyana risked antagonizing the major conservative power in the region, the United States, and allied itself with revolutionary forces. In both dismantling the ownership structure of the domestic economy and in its foreign policy initiatives, the Burnham government made a clean break with colonialism. Expatriate ownership of the economy was terminated, as was an unquestioning acceptance of the foreign policy positions of the advanced capitalist nations.

Whether what has gone on in Guyana represents a movement to socialism is to some extent a question of definition. Certainly there is a long tradition which identifies the public ownership of the means of production with socialism. By this criterion, Guyana might be considered a socialist nation. Yet at least from a Marxist point of view, there is a grave weakness in such a definition. A single-minded concern with the role of the public sector in the economy means that insufficient attention is paid, in the definition, to the class composition of that government. This, then, tends to mean that an inadequate analysis is made of government's role in influencing the class structure of the society. In the Marxist tradition, socialism is defined not merely as the public ownership of the economy; present also must be a government dominated by working class interests. By this standard, the government itself would have to be scrutinized before its acts of nationalization could be said to represent a movement of socialism. The advantage of this approach lies in the fact that it facilitates an analysis of the class relations and conflicts which emerge subsequent to the acts of nationalization.

In employing the Marxist criterion, it is unlikely that Guyana can be considered a socialist society. The adoption of "socialism" in Guyana was wholly an administrative matter undertaken by the ruling party and government. Almost no change in the officials of the government party, the People's National Congress (PNC) nor in the personnel of government occurred at the time of transition. No intensive period of ideological debate took place, nor did the change evoke a strong reaction along class lines in the country. The trajectory of the society was changed, but not under the initiative of the country's workers and farmers. In fact, the number of people who actually initiated this change was extremely small.

The transition to "socialism" reflected the pursuit of self-interest by a group of lawyers, teachers, professionals, and small businessmen – who came to political office with Independence. Fundamental to this situation was the fact that this class of political leaders had no direct economic interest in the dominant industries in Guyana. Both sugar and bauxite were foreign-owned. Thus, the institutional base for their power was not economic, but rather in their control of the state apparatus. Under these circumstances the bias of their rule was towards centralization. For in vesting increased control in the hands of the state, this class would, through their positions in government, also accumulate increased influence and power.[7]

In this way such seemingly radical acts as nationalization of foreign firms were attractive to the new leadership. The multinational firms in bauxite and sugar were seen as failing to contribute adequately to national development. They repatriated their profits, failed to invest sufficiently and, in the case of bauxite, did not diversify the range of their output. Furthermore, they represented sources of power beyond the control of indigenous leaders. As such they became obvious targets of government's policy.

It is plausible to argue that perhaps what the government might have done under these circumstances would be to buy out such firms and then auction them off to local businessmen. But such an action would run precisely counter to the centralizing bias of the government noted above. With much merit, public officials could argue that neither the financial strength nor technical competence to run such large firms were present within the local private sector. As a result, state ownership was the only arrangement by which such firms could be maintained as functioning enterprises.

When the nationalizations occurred, they were described as part of a "socialist thrust." In employing such an ideological defense for their actions, government officials were able to capture the positive benefits to be derived from identifying themselves as socialists. At the same time, they were able to avoid having to defend acts of nationalization on the much less attractive ground that such acts were part of the process by which a local governing class was extending and solidifying its base of power.

Evidence that workers have failed to capture power in Guyana is found most abundantly in the nationalized sector. In all state-owned enterprises, traditional hierarchical methods of decision-making have remained firmly in place. In none of the nationalized industries has meaningful workers' participation in decision-making been institutionalized. Nothing like the Yugoslav model of worker self-management has been introduced. What in effect has happened, especially in sugar and bauxite, is that new state based decision-makers are now filling managerial positions whose job descriptions have remained essentially unchanged with nationalization. To be sure, in some cases the actual decisions they make will differ from those made by the expatriate managers of the colonial era. Present-day management will, no doubt, make a much greater effort, in the bauxite industry for example, to purchase inputs locally and greater efforts than in the past will be made to diversify production of the sugar estates. But the point, precisely, is that the decision to make these initiatives has remained in managerial hands. The workers in the public sector industries are not integral participants in policy-making processes.

The foreclosing of worker participation in decision-making has important implications for the other two criteria by which we can determine whether management is using the state sector for self-advancement. In the absence of worker involvement, there simply is no mechanism present to counter tendencies to self-aggrandizement which may develop. Management in state corporations will be under constant temptation with regard to self-advancement, either through the dispensation of inordinantly high salaries and perquisites or through the letting of contracts to specially favored suppliers. The tendency to succumb to such particularistic as opposed to universalistic and economically rational criteria in allocating resources must be assumed to be omnipresent. Obviously there are no firm data available with regard to the extent that favored firms are the beneficiaries of corruption or that disproportionate wealth accrues to managers. But the failure to implement schemes by which managerial prerogatives are constrained or at least opened to workers and public scrutiny cannot help but raise the suspicion that private appropriation for personal gain is occurring.

The absence of schemes of worker self-management thus represents in itself partial evidence of the emergence of a state-based managerial class. So, too, does the behavior of the Guyanese working class. Especially in the period since the wave of nationalizations, strike activity has been frequent and bitter. Both sugar and bauxite have been the object of intense, and in the case of sugar, prolonged strikes. No data are available for strike days lost in the public sector in recent years, but such actions have been frequent. In an admittedly atypical week in December 1977, strikes or slowdowns affected state-owned ferries, buses, the airline and airport, electricity corporations, the water company, rice board, pharmaceutical corporation and postal service. At the same time the sugar industry was involved in a strike which exceeded four months in duration. It is furthermore significant that much of the strike activity which has occurred, especially in bauxite and sugar, centers on the issue of the extent to which industry profits should be shared with the work force. This, of course, exactly parallels the focus of class struggle in capitalist economies. The antagonism between management and labor which this strike activity symbolizes therefore suggests the resumption of the pattern of class relations made familiar by capitalism.

It is important to make a similar analysis of the cooperative sector. For, as we have seen, the Burnham government has argued that the transition to socialism will be accomplished primarily through cooperatives. Even though the state sector dwarfs the cooperative sector in economic importance, the cooperatives are institutions of particular concern to government. It is thus important to evaluate the extent to which capitalist or socialist relations are encouraged in this way.

The evaluation of the cooperative sector is similar to that of the state sector. The PNC's Code of Conduct does not even require that financial interests in cooperative societies be listed. Since there is no possibility of public scrutiny of such involvement, the coooperative sector becomes especially subject to what Clive Thomas has called "bureaucratic dispensation."[9] In the absence of either public or worker involvement in the decision-making process, and in the absence of a requirement that personal involvement in cooperatives be made public it is all too easy to see how a government manager could use his or her position for personal self-advancement. Thus it is at least possible, especially in fields such as building and construction where government purchases are significant, that the cooperative sector acts essentially to facilitate personal wealth appropriation by erstwhile state employees.

Above and beyond this issue, there is also the question of the internal organization of the cooperatives and the extent to which they contain socialist productive relations. If they do, at least a plausible case could be made that by encouraging cooperative societies, government is, in fact, speeding the diffusion of socialism. The problem is that what looks like and is called a cooperative may actually be organized no differently than a private capitalist firm. Commercial success might allow cooperatives to expand the scale of their operation. If they do so by hiring wage labor rather than by allowing new memberships to be created in the cooperative the essential class relations of a capitalist firm will be replicated. It is this concern which must have motivated the Bolsheviks in their rejection of Bukharin's thesis that cooperatives could help introduce socialism into the country-side. The problem is that cooperatives can adapt to their environment. The role they play therefore will be heavily influenced by the policies which are established to guide their development. Minimally, therefore a government interested in using cooperatives to spread socialism would have to move decisively to curb expansion through the hiring of wage labor.

The problem of wage labor in the cooperative sector in Guyana has not received official attention. However, it is clear that by its silence government assents to its use. Indeed, the most successful cooperative societies such as the Cooperative Wholesale Complex and the various cooperatives in the building and construction industry use wage labor extensively. Not coincidently, strike activity against the cooperatives has occurred in both cases. From the point of view of the wage worker especially, and the society generally, it is hard to discern the difference between labor-hiring cooperatives and labor-hiring corporations. Thus it is easy to argue that without constraints on the hiring of wage earners, the spread of cooperatives in Guyana represents a form of the extension of capitalism.

The pattern of change and continuity in post-colonial Guyana, then, can be summarized in the following way. The country's foreign policy and the ownership structure of its economy have been radically altered. At the same time, the conditions under which production is now carried on remains traditionally hierarchical even though undertaken within cooperative or state structures. It is thus clear that Guyana has experienced a profound process of decolonization. It has not, however, embarked upon the transition to socialism. The older colonial ruling class and its business firms have been banished and decision-making power now rests with a local elite of state and cooperative-based managers. In the Guyanese context this assumes the form of the emergence of an urban Afro-Guyanese leadership under the auspices of the People's National Congress (PNC). It excludes both the rural and urban proletariats, although a substantial section of the latter, who are Afro-Guyanese in extraction, at least in the past provided electoral support to the PNC. Decolonization has then allowed a new ruling class to emerge. Primarily using the state sector, they have forged, for the first time, a local economic foundation for political power.

A militant foreign policy, nationalization, development of cooperatives, and even the invocation of socialist ideology are all very important aspects of Guyanese reality. But what none of these, in the end, represents is the advance to power of the Guyanese working class and peasantry. To be sure, the functioning of the Guyanese economy especially with its predominant state sector is very different from that of a conventional capitalist economy. In light of that the term "state capitalism" best designates Guyana's current mode of production.

With the onset of state capitalism the burden of promoting economic development falls predominantly onto the public sector. The adopting of this new economic structure in Guyana has two important dimensions. On one hand, as we have seen, it provides the economic undergirding for the emergence of a new class rule in the country. At the same time it vests directly in these state administrators and officials the responsibility for the country's efforts to achieve economic development. Quite specifically, this means that the new ruling class will be judged with respect to its success in increasing the volume of output and the productivity of the Guyanese economy.

As we saw in the first chapters the development process is one in which output increases and becomes diversified as a result of technological advance. Conceived in its broadest terms, then, success in promoting economic development necessitates the creation of an environment in which innovative behavior both with regard to production methods and the range of outputs is encouraged. This means that decision-makers must be motivated to search for alternatives in production methods and to experiment with new products. It also means that when such decision-makers do these things, the appropriate stock of knowledge and information must be available to them. Producers under an appropriate incentive system who are able to call upon a relevant fund of information are those who will be able to implement the innovative decisions integral to the development process.

In international capitalism, new technology frequently is carried to developing countries by multinational firms; it is not generated in a local capital goods industry. The anticipation on the part of such countries is that by encouraging this investment, the handicaps associated with the absence of scientific and engineering personnel can be minimized. The presumption also is that with the investment by the multinational firms, local personnel will be trained and familiarized with advanced techniques. Ultimately it is hoped that this process will reduce the supply side constraints to the development of an indigenous technology which required the presence of international firms in the first place.

The solution to the problem of technological dynamism is altogether different for a state capitalist nation like Guyana that cannot rely on foreign capital. Increased levels of productivity for such a country must be generated internally. The identification and adoption of new methods of production and outputs under such circumstances will rest entirely with state-based indigenous managers, engineers and scientists. Similarly, the incentive system by which a search for technological advance is generated must be directed to the appropriate public sector staff. Since foreign investment cannot be the engine of technological advance, a country in Guyana's circumstances must therefore be even more careful to ensure that the skills and motivations for the difficult task of implementing technological advance are present, than, for example, a nation which uses methods of production already developed abroad. Quite specifically this means as we have seen that such a nation must either develop its own capital goods industry, or else ensure that its agricultural sector is sufficiently dynamic to allow for the importation of needed capital goods. Failing both of these and having shut itself off from international investment, a country will be doomed to technological stagnation and failure in its development efforts.

By any measure, Guyana's experience in promoting economic development in the last decade has been distinctly disappointing. Tables 9.1 and 9.2 provide information with respect to both the volume and composition of output over the period from the mid-1960s to the 1980. In both cases the picture which emerges is one of stagnation and stability, whereas a pattern

Table 9.1

INDEXES OF PHYSICAL OUTPUT GUYANESE AGRICULTURE, MINING AND QUARRYING, AND MANUFACTURING, 1966–1980 (1972 = 100)

Year	Agriculture	Mining and Quarrying	Manufacturing
1966	90.3	89.0	73.5
1967	99.3	88.1	81.1
1968	94.5	97.4	76.8
1969	102.9	106.2	72.1
1970	100.1	114.4	81.4
1971	109.7	111.8	92.7
1972	100.0	100.0	100.0
1973	96.0	95.2	107.3
1974	112.7	102.9	123.3
1975	103.4	104.6	119.9
1976	117.0	106.2	124.9
1977[a]	108.9	93.4	97.2
1978[a]	116.5	79.7	108.4
1979[a]	107.1	74.0	109.0
1980[a]	105.7	79.9	N.A.

Revised and calculated from the source: Computed from Bank of Guyana, *1980 Annual Report*, Table VIII, 1.

[a] Provisional.

of development would be reflected in growth and dynamism in these measures.[10]

The indexes reported in Table 9.1 show how little the economy grew in this period. Only manufacturing output grew steadily in this period. But as we shall see in Table 9.2, despite this growth, manufacturing remained as a miniscule proportion of the Guyanese economy. From such a small base almost any growth at all would show up as a large percentage increment. Even so, almost one-half of the value of manufacturing is accounted for by rum production, a by-product, of course, of sugar. Agriculture and mining and quarrying, by far the most important sectors of the economy, saw much lower rates of growth. Agriculture's performance was erratic, with output at

Table 9.2

PERCENTAGE SECTORAL CONTRIBUTIONS TO GUYANESE GROSS DOMESTIC PRODUCT 1966, 1980

	1966	1980[1]
Sugar	12.5	14.8
Rice	5.7	3.8
Livestock	2.2	3.1
Other Agriculture	2.9	3.6
Total Agriculture	23.3	25.3
Manufacturing	7.7	8.0
Engineering and Construction	6.4	6.7
Fishing	1.4	1.3
Forestry	1.8	1.2
Mining and Quarrying	7.7	8.0
Services	38.9	30.8
Government	12.8	18.7

[1] Provisional revised and calculated from: Bank of Guyana, *Annual Report*, 1976, 1980, Table VIII, 6.

a peak in 1976 about 17 percent higher than that of 1972, but declining in the following year to a level, in 1980, only about 6 percent higher than the base year. Physical output of the bauxite-dominated sector, on the other hand, crested in 1970. Since then output has declined with 1979's level of output almost 26 percent below the level reached in that peak year and 1980's level more than 20 percent below production in 1970.

When we turn to the structure of production, in Table 9.2, we observe a comparable pattern of stagnation. Agriculture's percentage contribution to output remained steady at about one-fourth of the economy. At the same time manufacturing made no advance, remaining in the vicinity of only about 8 percent of the gross domestic product. Similarly engineering and construction, a sector which would have grown if capital goods production were increasing in importance, also remained stable at only about 6 percent of the gross domestic product. The poor output performance of mining and quarrying also shows up as stability in its proportional contribution to output. Only government during this period experienced a substantial relative advance, increasing its contribution to almost one-fifth by 1980.

In combination these two tables reveal an economy which still has not broken out of the pattern inherited from colonialism. The traditional agricultural export orientation is present, rapid expansion is not occurring, and dynamic new sources of production are not emerging. This stability in economic performance, of course, stands in sharp contrast to the dramatic changes which have occurred in the economy's ownership structure. With economic development at the forefront of the goals of the government, the movement to nationalization should have facilitated the implementation of policies to accomplish that end. Yet such achievements are not revealed in the data. This raises the question of why the increased role of the state in the Guyanese economy has not been development-promoting.

Symbolic of what has gone wrong in Guyana is the experience of agriculture in general and sugar in particular. All observers, including the government, agree that Guyanese development necessitates agricultural expansion and rationalization. Such a program is necessary to curb imports, raise incomes and stimulate technological change. To achieve this end, however, a close collaborative relationship between the government and the agricultural working class is necessary. Only by involving the rural workers in decisions with respect to the output mix and methods of cultivation can be government tap the good will of this group. In doing that, the rationale for shifting to new crops and new methods of production could be made clear to the workers, a process of explanation which would facilitate such a transition. A mutually acceptable incentive system for encouraging this shift, once agreed upon, would encourage the process of agricultural modernization. With a spirit of cooperation and mutual trust a positive environment could be constructed, one which would be important in allowing agriculture to become a leading sector of economic development.

Indeed, in the immediate aftermath of that nationalization of sugar, it appeared possible that such a fruitful relationship might emerge and the traditional management/labor hostility in the sugar industry might lessen. Official recognition was granted to the Guyana Agricultural and General Workers Union (GAWU), a union which is closely related to the opposition People's Progressive Party (PPP). This union has long demonstrated its ability to command the loyalty of the sugar workers, despite the fact that never before had it received official sanction as the bargaining agent in the industry. Recognition of the GAWU seemed to signal a new era in industrial relations in the sugar industry, one which seemed to auger well for efforts achieve productivity advances in the industry.

Such a positive trend did not, however, prevail for long. Paralleling a deterioration in relations between the dominant political parties, relations between the sugar industry's management and workers deteriorated abruptly in 1977. The failure of government to implement a profit-sharing scheme triggered a strike during the second harvest of 1977 which, by the time it ended, had lasted 135 days. When the strike finally was called off, the issues separating the government and the workers still had not been resolved. But in its residue intense emotions lingered, indicating that difficulties awaited the government in its effort to enlist the cooperation of the sugar workers in implementing plans to raise levels of labor productivity in the industry.

Fundamentally at issue here is the nature of the PNC government. Briefly put, it is a regime which is manager-dominated, urban, and predominantly Afro-Guyanese. The peasant and agricultural section of the population – largely of Indo-Guyanese descent – is inadequately represented within the government's ranks.[11] As a result, the ruling party and the government is poorly equipped either to mobilize the rural labor force or to call upon its good will in attempting to transform agriculture. Conversely, the groups among whom the government does possess a suitable organizational infrastructure are not farmers and at best have only a marginal relationship to agriculture. Thus they are of little relevance in a strategy of agricultural modernization.

The PNC government deliberately and quite explicitly has ruled out the possibility of governing in coalition with the PPP, the party supported by the bulk of the rural population. Paradoxically the PNC's determination not to share power with the PPP and through it Guyana's agricultural labor force exists despite the fact that both parties, at least nominally, share socialist goals.

The estrangement between the rural Indo-Guyanese community and the PNC dates from the late 1950s when the latter was formed as a result of a split in the PPP. Especially in the years of internal self-rule, 1961–1964, when the PPP was in office, it was accused by the PNC of being a "rice" government. In levelling this charge the PNC meant that the PPP paid excessive attention to agriculture, investing too much money, for example, in drainage and irrigation projects. It was argued that money thus spent in the countryside benefitted the PPP's own rural constituency at the expense of the urban population. This was used as an effective rallying cry by the PNC in mobilizing its own urban political base, but in the process it thereby antagonized the PPP's rural constituency. With its accession to power in 1964 the PNC in fact substantially lowered the priority claim to resources which the PPP government had assigned to agriculture.

What all of this means is that now, when the PNC government is increasingly conscious of the important role agriculture must play in Guyanese development, it is ill-equipped to do anything about it. The government increasingly exhorts the population to "grow more food" and to "feed, clothe, and house" itself. But as we have seen, such exhortations have not produced tangible results in agricultural production statistics. Ultimately, the source of this failure is rooted in the fact that the government lacks organization and credibility among the rural Indo-Guyanese population.

As a result of this, programs for agriculture have assumed an *ad hoc* and, at times, a desperate quality. The latter is exemplified by a government scheme in late 1977 and early 1978 to redeploy urban, largely Afro-Guyanese civil servants to the status of cane cutters, in an effort to secure a more acquiescent labor force in agriculture. But the issue of mobilizing agriculture clearly will not be resolved by attempting in such a way to by-pass the interests and concerns of the population already resident in the countryside. A resolution of the estrangement between city and countryside – and in the Guyanese context this means a resolution of the estrangement between Afro-Guyanese and Indo-Guyanese – awaits a political solution. Until this division is satisfactorily healed, government efforts in agriculture will be hamstrung because of its inability to call upon the good will and energies of the farm population. Development, in short, in Guyana requires priority attention to agriculture, but that in turn necessitates political authority deeply rooted in the countryside. This the current government lacks.

The problem which this necessity raises, however, goes to the root of Guyana's post-colonial mode of production. It thus raises the question of whether Guyana, as currently structured, is capable of generating modern economic growth. For if the current analysis is accurate, nothing less than a redefinition of the relationship between the state-based elite and the country's agricultural workers is required to achieve development. If not actually representing the accession to power of the rural labor force, such a redefinition would certainly require a diminution in the unquestioned authority presently enjoyed by the current governing class. Economic development in Guyana, in short, requires, if not socialism, then at least a mode of production which permits a wider diffusion of power and authority than currently exists.

On the present evidence it is hard to envision the currently dominant regime voluntarily initiating such a redefinition and diffusion of authority. Whether such a sharing of power does emerge in Guyana will, therefore, depend upon the extent to which it is compelled by the Guyanese people. Our analysis indicates that it is upon the strength and efficacy of that demand that the country's hopes for economic development rest.

A summary statement of the hypothesis suggested in this chapter is that the political leaders of independent Guyana, exercising the political autonomy present in a post-colonial setting, have restructured Guyanese society. In the process they have provided for themselves, in an enhanced state sector, the economic underpinnings to their continued rule but have not, as a result, started the construction of socialism. The fact, however, that this new state-based ruling class is largely urban and of Afro-Guyanese descent, has meant that it is poorly equipped to promote successfully the country's economic development. A successful development strategy in Guyana depends on the harnessing of the energies of the agricultural work force. To date, the country does not possess a government capable of making that critical linkage.

NOTES

1. Ministry of Economic Development, *Economic Survey of Guyana 1973*, p. 40.
2. See my "Problems of the Noncapitalist Path of Development in Guyana and Jamaica," in *Politics and Society*, Vol. 7, No. 2 (1977).
3. "Declaration of Sophia" (Address by the Leader of the People's National Congress, Prime Minister Forbes Burnham, at a Special Congress to Mark the Tenth Anniversary of the PNC in Government, December 14, 1974), pp. 12, 17.
4. *Constitution*, People's National Congress, p. 1.
5. Burnham, "Declaration of Sophia."
6. Ministry of Co-operatives and National Mobilization, "Growth of Co-operative Movement, 1948–1975."
7. A similar phenomenon has been noted by Hamza Alavi in his "The State in Post-Colonial Societies," *New Left Review*, Vol. 74, July/August (1972). See also Michaela von Freyhold, "The Post-Colonial State and Its Tanzanian Version," *Review of African Political Economy*, No. 8; Colin Ley, "The 'Over-developed' Post-Colonial State: A Re-evaluation," *Review of African Political Economy*, No. 5; and John Saul, "The State in Post-Colonial Societies – Tanzania," *The Socialist Register 1973* (London, 1974).
8. In its Code of Conduct the PNC requires government officials to declare their financial interests. However the Prime Minister has recently announced that these declarations are not to be made public. See *Sunday Chronicle*, May 21, 1978.
9. Clive Y. Thomas, "Non-capitalist Development as Theory and Practice of Decolonization and Socialist Transformation." Paper presented to the *Colloquium on Comparative Studies of Decolonization and Dependence*, University of California, Berkeley, December 2, 1976, p. 27.
10. In Table 9.1, we employ index of physical output rather than the more conventional national income and product account data for two reasons: first, no reliable consumer price index exists by which to deflate the current dollar estimates of these measures; second, because of the phenomenal, but temporary increase in the price of sugar which occurred on world markets in 1974 and 1975, the country's gross domestic product figures for these years reflect a misleading increase.
11. See Ralph R. Premdas, "Elections and Political Campaigns in a Racially Bifurcated State: The Case of Guyana," *The Journal of Inter-American Studies and World Affairs*, Vol. 14, No. 3 (1972).

Chapter 10

Petro-Development in Trinidad and Tobago

While Guyana and Jamaica were experimenting with versions of socialism the country of Trinidad and Tobago was embarked upon a much more traditional approach to development. Under the leadership of Prime Minister Eric Williams, Trinidad and Tobago resolutely set itself in opposition to Leftist currents in the region. In terms of development strategy this conservatism primarily took the form of continued efforts to attract private investment capital from abroad. Even so, as we shall see, Trinidad and Tobago's approach was not identical to that of the 1950s and 1960s. In particular, the government was called upon to play a much more active role in the economy than in classic dependency – an expanded role which was feasible since the country benefitted from its position as petroleum producer and exporter.

Trinidad and Tobago is the country in the economically most advantageous position in the region. As an oil producing country, though not a member of OPEC, it has been the beneficiary of the huge increase in petroleum prices which has occurred in the years after 1973. The revenue generated from this source eliminated at least in the short-run financing as a constraint to the country's economic expansion. In Trinidad and Tobago the question of development centered chiefly on whether the society would deploy its new found wealth in a way to expand efficiently its long-term capacity to produce a diversified and expanded level of output.

The magnitude of Trinidad and Tobago's gain as a result of the increase in petroleum prices borders on the unbelievable. In 1973 the contribution of the country's mining sector, almost exclusively petroleum, to the Gross Domestic Product was $454.7 million (TT). In the very next year this contribution had increased more than threefold to $1,477.8 million (TT). And again in 1975 this contribution increased by another 53 percent to $2,269.8 million (TT). By 1977 the mining sector contributed almost $3,000.0 million (TT) to Trinidad's economy, more than six times the level it had in 1973. It was, of course, this phenomenal increase which primarily was responsible for the fact that over these years Trinidad and Tobago's Gross Domestic Production, in current prices, increased almost threefold.[1] In 1970 the per capita Gross Domestic Product of Trinidad and Tobago and Jamaica had been roughly comparable, while that of Barbados was of the same order of magnitude. By 1978 Trinidad and Tobago's per capita GDP far outdistanced that of the other countries of the region. (See Table 10.1)

Table 10.1

PER CAPITA GROSS DOMESTIC PRODUCT, COUNTRIES OF THE CARIBBEAN, 1970, 1977

Country	1970	1977
Barbados	$606	$1,770
Guyana	329	520
Jamaica	750	1,060
Trinidad and Tobago	790	2,620

Revised and calculated from the source: The World Bank, *World Bank Tables*, 2nd ed., 1980, pp. 1, 38, 94, 114, 198.

Indeed, Trinidad and Tobago ranked twenty-eighth in the world in this measure ahead of such countries as Yugoslavia, Argentina and Portugal, as well as Hong Kong and Puerto Rico.[2]

As yet, however, the income growth experienced in the country has not resulted in economic development. There has been a growth in per capita income, but, in following Kuznets, an expansion in that measure is not the sole criterion to be employed when assessing whether development has occurred in a country. In addition it is necessary to determine whether the application of modern technology has resulted in an expansion in the array of outputs produced in the country.

When looked at in this light the situation in Trinidad and Tobago is much less favorable than would initially appear to be the case. For example the value of manufacturing output in the country actually was higher in 1970 than it was in 1977 and seems to have peaked in 1972. Similarly the value of agricultural output was only about the same in 1977 as it had been in 1970, again having peaked in 1972.[3] Indeed it is only a slight exaggeration to suggest that Trinidad and Tobago in the 1970s had become a monocultural economy. Petroleum dominated the economy at the expense of all else.

There has long been a concern in Trinidad and Tobago that just such a lop-sided economy would emerge. Principally this anxiety took the form of expressions of doubt that the local capitalist class would prove capable of initiating an industrialization effort. As early as 1968 the government voiced concern that the nation's private sector would not contribute adequately to the development process. It specifically warned that "any failure on the part of the private sector to perform should be attributed to a failure to seize the numerous investment opportunities in the country." Again in 1973 an official publication declared that

> in spite of generous fiscal concessions, because of innate deficiencies in the private sector that sector could not be relied upon alone to produce the kind of momentum which the country required to safeguard its economic independence and provide for additional jobs, economic growth and an equitable distribution of national income.[4]

The data cited earlier on manufacturing output tend to support this critique and suggest that what the government sector had to say about the local private sector in the 1960s retains its validity.

Andrew S. Richter, in his study of decision-making in the country, is in essential agreement with the judgment concerning the capacity of the local business class. He notes that Trinidadian businessmen have exhibited a very cautious attitude toward investment, never straying very far from their initial mercantile, rather than industrial, interests. Richter concedes that the huge capital outlays required in the petroleum sector are beyond their capacities. But even in smaller scale manufacturing Richter writes, "local business interest goes no further than the same low local value-added import-substituting assembly project." In this regard he contrasts the attitudes of local businesses with foreign firms: "Whether in petroleum or manufacturing MNC's in Trinidad have been oriented towards exporting. The local private sector, whether in commerce or in assembling industries, is oriented towards importing."[5]

Great doubt thus exists with regard to the capacity of indigenous private businesses to implement the industrialization process. As Richter puts it, "industrialism cannot proceed without industrialists."[6] It is in this context that the government of Trinidad and Tobago has encouraged multinational corporations to play a significant role in Trinidad and Tobago's economy and in fact to create and dominate its manufacturing sector. Just such a situation has developed. Between 1966 and 1976 almost 60 percent of the manufacturing sector of the economy was owned by foreign investors accounting for between 15 and 20 percent of the country's GDP. By way of contrast almost all of the trade sector, was owned by nationals and made a similar contribution to the country's economy.[7]

But though foreign investors were to play an important role, the strategy of development pursued by the government of Eric Williams was not identical to the dependent development approach employed in the 1950s and 1960s. The government was accountable for the performance of the economy and thus could not afford to abdicate total responsibility for decision-making to foreign corporations. If the decisions made by the latter were undesirable from Trinidad and Tobago's point of view it was the political leaders not the corporations who would be held responsible. In this setting government officials possessed an incentive to use the public sector to influence private economic decisions.

Not only was there the incentive to do so, but especially after 1973 the government also possessed the financial capability to undertake such an activist role. Between 1973 and 1974 alone total government revenue more than doubled, 90 percent of which came from the petroleum sector.[8] Even before 1973 the Williams government had envisioned for itself an activist role in an essentially private economy. But after the 1973 windfall, this approach became increasingly feasible.

In 1974 an official statement declared that the additional foreign reserves which the government now possessed place it "in a better position to diversify the structure of the economy."[9]

It intended, the statement went on, to do this through a strategy of national participation. Foreign investors would be expected to join with nationals as equity partners in their investment projects. But it was assumed that the local private sector would only make a minor contribution in this regard. As a result the strategy of participation actually envisioned the government, as representative of national interests, joining with foreign private investors in creating new manufacturing sectors of the economy. This the government would be able to do by using the revenues generated by petroleum.[10]

With this policy of participation – especially public sector participation – prospective new foreign investors were required to secure the good will of government. In effect, would-be investors were compelled to seek out government as a willing partner. In this approach government was positioned to pass judgment on all potential projects and separate those which it desired from those which it did not. In this way, it was anticipated, the officials of the government would be able to influence the sectoral distribution of such investment and the degree of labor utilization present in such projects and thus maximally benefit the local economy. In support of this goal the government drew up a list of schemes which it hoped would come alive in this way. Projected for the future in Trinidad were such industries as steel, aluminum smelting, fertilizer and petrochemical industries, additional oil refining capacity, feedstock and several others. In each case it was projected that a public/foreign-private joint venture would be created.

With the rise in the price of petroleum, steps in this direction were implemented at once. As Richter has noted "by 1975 [public] participation was a fact of life in Trinidad and it seems likely that it will continue to be so." As he summarizes the government strategy, government would do

> what national private investors had declined to do: create a mature economy through industrialization. Foreign rather than national private investors would play a key role and government's participation would help to insure that the MNC's role did not run counter to national interests and goals.[11]

It is, of course, too early to judge the success of Trinidad and Tobago's development strategy. It is possible that the country may be able to attract capital, in sufficient volume, to allow it to achieve a substantial degree of industrialization. It is conceivable that the government's equity role may provide it with sufficient influence so as to minimize the harmful effects and maximize the beneficial results of such investment. But for this approach to work government's influencing function itself must be effective. Beneficial projects must be pursued and encouraged and brought to fruition. Projects with little benefit for the country should be discouraged.

A question therefore which suggests itself in this connection concerns the competency of Trinidad's government bureaucracy. In this strategy the governmental role is substantial and therefore the scope for error is large. To an important extent efficiency and expertise in the public sector is an important element in Trinidad and Tobago's approach to industrialization. But simply to raise the question of the competence of government administration, in the West Indian context, is to raise a host of doubts. Thus, in a generally favorable examination of the public service machinery in the region, Garcia-Zamor notes that

> ... without exception, the planning, budgeting, and executing agencies suffer from problems of recruitment and retention of middle level personnel ... [a shortcoming which] seriously hampers the countries' development capacity.[12]

The fundamental issue here is whether, as decision-making power devolves on the public sector, the latter is acquiring the enhanced capability necessary to carry out the tasks of development. To date most Caribbean commentators would, following Garcia-Zamor, answer this question in the negative, suggesting that the Trinidad path to industrialization may not be as smooth as it could be if adequate expertise and motivation were present in the public sector.

The combination of a relatively weak public sector bureaucracy and the favorable investment climate created by the conservatism of Trinidad's government suggests the possibility that investors in the country may not be subject to as much control as the government's policy statements suggest they might be. It is conspicuously the case that specific guidelines for policymakers have not been publicly announced. There is thus wide latitude for discretion – not to mention corruption – in the way officials rule on the suitability of projects. The possibility arises, then, that the country may become the host for large volumes of but barely controlled investment from abroad.

At a more fundamental level questions can be raised concerning the viability of the design of Trinidad and Tobago's development strategy. Doubts suggest themselves over the question of whether it is possible for the government of a small country like Trinidad and Tobago to exercise effective control over the behavior of multinational corporations within its borders. C. Y. Thomas has made the negative case. He writes that a program of majority state participation such as that proposed for Trinidad and Tobago rests on a "basic misunderstanding of what a multinational corporation, and particularly an exporting corporation represents locally." He writes:

> It is essentially a plant. It is not a firm. It is true that there are titles such as Directors, Managers, Managing Directors, etc. But the local expression . . . makes no decisions as regards prices . . . output . . . levels of investment, or the markets. All these are done at the head office, where decisions which normally define a firm are made. The apparatus which exists locally is just a participant in a multi-plant firm.

From this he concludes that even with majority state ownership of the enterprise "there will inevitably be little change in the content and methods of production."[13]

If Thomas is correct in this analysis then the rationale for Trinidad and Tobago's state majority participation is undermined. It will be recalled that the justification for that program was that it would enable the government to influence managerial decisions and in this way curb or eliminate harmful effects from the activities of the international firm. But Thomas argues that, in fact, managerial decisions are not made on the local level in branch plant activities. There are thus few decisions which can be influenced in the way suggested by the government and therefore little scope available for the kind of influence anticipated by the official position.

Seen in a different light, however, state equity participation may be viewed not as a tool to overcome the problems associated with dependent development, but rather as a means of augmenting that approach to development. In this regard Trinidad's chances for success seem reasonably bright. With the Government of Trinidad an associated partner substantial advantages accrue to a would-be investor. Primarily these advantages center on the question of risk and uncertainty. A prospective investor, promised the participation of the state in an industrial project, can be reasonably certain that public policy will be favorable to it. Implementation of tax or import policies which would negatively impinge on the profitability or efficiency of such an enterprise is not likely where the policymakers themselves have a stake in the financial success of the firm. This, of course, would precisely be the case where public joint ventures are present. In addition, state investment reduces the capital outlay required by the multinational firm. With less at stake, all other things held constant, a firm is more likely to invest than where it is required to undertake the entire financing of an industrial project. To be sure this advantage to some extent is offset by the prospect of the firm's having to share profits with the public sector. But this negative factor in all likelihood is not strong enough typically to offset the benefits which flow from government's possessing an equity share. This is all the more so, precisely, as Thomas argues, because it is unlikely that the public sector will be able decisively to influence managerial decisions. The result is that the firm will be relatively unimpeded in pursuing its goals, safe in an environment in which government, because it is an important shareholder, protects its interests.

State equity participation thus can be seen as a means of attracting direct private foreign investment. In practice, if not intention, it is not so much a policy to control international firms as it is to reduce their concerns and anxieties. It is a technique to be employed in a strategy of development where the intention is to encourage the flow of capital into the country. In this regard wealth produces wealth. For if government investment is helpful in attracting capital, the government must be able to meet the financial requirements of such investment. This is precisely where Trinidad and Tobago found itself in an attractive situation. Its petroleum wealth positioned it better than any other country in the region to offer terms which would attract foreign investment and advance the strategy of dependent development.

In light of all of the above it is possible to hypothesize the likely future of Trinidad and Tobago's development. The country's stable and hospitable investment climate should ensure that it will continue to be the recipient of capital inflows from abroad. The role of the state as an equity partner in industrial projects should serve further to enhance the attractiveness of the country to investors. At the same time the relative inefficiency of the public administration in Trinidad and Tobago suggests that few effective limitations or controls will be imposed on such investors, even if the government were willing to risk its growth strategy by adopting such policies. In any event following Thomas, the actual scope for such limitations is very much in doubt. It is likely, therefore, that the country will be successful in achieving a central end of its development strategy – the securing of investment from abroad – but without being able to implement the safeguards which the government itself has emphasized are important.

Further economic development can thus be anticipated in Trinidad and Tobago. But, of course, the question which remains open even after it is acknowledged that dependent development may occur is whether and how successful this development experience will be in reducing poverty and eliminating unemployment. For, in the end, the capability of satisfying the needs of the population will be the test against which Trinidad's development strategy will be measured. It is with regard to this question that it is not possible to be optimistic.

It is likely that indigenous businesses will not in the future play a central role in the development process. The task of organizing production and creating jobs will, in Trinidad and Tobago's approach, fall largely into the hands of foreign investors in concert with the government. As a result the principal means by which the Trinidad population can benefit from the development occurring in the country is by receiving the wages and salaries paid for the new jobs which come into existence. That there is a need both for income and jobs is clear. A 1972 survey revealed, for example, that 85.6 percent of households in the country received annually less than $500

(TT).[14] Furthermore as Trevor M. A. Farrell has pointed out in an article published in 1978 "unemployment is high and in terms of the numbers unemployed, it has risen more or less steadily over the last thirty years."[15] For the government, therefore, to claim success in the economy it must not only be able to show that economic development is progressing but, as well, that human welfare, at least as revealed in terms of household income and a declining unemployment rate, too is advancing.

The order of magnitude of what needs to be done for full employment to be achieved is revealed in a set of calculations performed by Farrell for the 1970–85 period. For this goal to be accomplished the rate of job creation would have to be more than double the rate achieved in the immediately preceding decade. While the annual rate of job creation between 1965 and 1974 was 1.4 percent per year, Farrell projects that for full employment to have been achieved by 1985 the rate of job creation will have to have increased to 3.2 percent per year.[16]

Farrell is skeptical that that rate of advance is feasible with the current approach. He notes that the country has benefitted from the petroleum windfall and that "many large projects are currently being mooted." But, he goes on, "experience justifies extreme skepticism as to how many of these will actually come on stream. Furthermore even if they do these projects are basically of a highly capital-intensive nature. . . . By themselves they promise to do little to solve the unemployment problem." In fact, Farrell speculates increasing capital intensity in association with a growth in the labor force may result in an increase in unemployment rather than a decrease.[17]

It is possible that Farrell is too pessimistic. It has been the burden of the argument presented here that conditions are changing in the country in a direction which may result in an increased volume of capital inflow. This could well mean an increase in the rate of job creation and presents the possibility of decreasing the country's unemployment rate, contrary to Farrell's expectations.

Yet at the same time there is no denying Farrell's emphasis on the limited job creating potential inherent in the country's approach to development. The technology imported to Trinidad and Tobago was developed in metropolitan country in response to input markets in which labor typically was expensive and capital relatively cheap. It therefore was biased away from the use of the former and to the latter. When brought to a country like Trinidad such a technology, even when modified, simply does not create many employment opportunities. A given level of foreign investment typically therefore will be disappointing in its job creating possibilities. As a result it too will be disappointing in its ability to reduce poverty in the country.

Under these circumstances it is likely that foreign private investment in Trinidad even if growing will do more for the country's gross domestic product than it will for its people. In this sense Trinidad's experience is likely to be similar to that of other developing capitalist as discussed in Chapter 3: the economy may prosper but the basic needs of much of its population may go unfulfilled.

NOTES

1. The World Bank, *World Bank Tables*, 2nd ed., 1980, pp. 198–199.
2. The World Bank, *World Development Report 1980* (New York: Oxford University Press, 1980), pp. 110–111.
3. The World Bank, *World Bank Tables*, pp. 198–199.
4. Andrew S. Richter, "Multinational Corporations, Local Businessmen and the State in a Small Developing Country: A Case Study of Trinidad and Tobago" (unpublished Ph.D. dissertation, Yale University, 1979), p. 141.
5. Richter, "Multinational Corporations," pp. 233, 235.
6. Richter, "Multinational Corporations," p. 235.
7. Richter, "Multinational Corporations," p. 143; The World Bank, *World Bank Tables*, p. 199.
8. Richter, "Multinational Corporations," p. 412.
9. *Review of the Economy, 1974* (Trinidad: Government Printery, 1974), p. 1.
10. See *White Paper No. 2 on Public Sector Participation in Industry* (Trinidad: Government Printery, 1979).
11. Richter, "Multinational Corporations," pp. 414, 141–142.
12. Jean Claude Garcia Zamor, *The Ecology of Development Administration in Jamaica, Trinidad and Tobago and Barbados* (Washington: General Secretariat, Organization of American States, 1977), p. 75.
13. Clive Y. Thomas, *Dependence and Transformation: The Economics of the Transition to Socialism* (New York: Monthly Review Press, 1974), pp. 95–96.
14. Computed from Richter, "Multinational Corporations," p. 132.

15. Trevor M. A. Farrell, "The Unemployment Crisis in Trinidad and Tobago: Its Current Dimensions and Some Projections to 1985," *Social and Economic Studies* 27, 2 (June 1978):121.
16. Farrell, "Unemployment Crisis," p. 147.
17. Farrell, "Unemployment Crisis," p. 149.

Chapter 11

Conclusion

The plantation economies of the English-speaking Caribbean were created as a result of European expansion. In that sense the West Indies always were part of the international capitalist economy. But internally they did not contain capitalist class relations. Their relations of production militated against technological change. As a result the region was denied the development process which was experienced in Europe and other regions where capitalism took root. As long as the plantation economy prevailed underdevelopment persisted.

With the ending of World War II the Caribbean entered into a new era. The plantation economy with its class relations based on coercion were dismantled and a capitalist class structure emerged. In turn, capitalist growth, largely dependent upon the importation of foreign capital was initiated. But the results of dependent capitalist growth varied in the three countries examined in this study. Guyana was the least successful in attracting private foreign investment, while Trinidad and Jamaica both experienced substantial advances in output, especially mineral output, undertaken by foreign interests. Trinidad in the 1970s particularly prospered as a result of the exceptional increase in petroleum prices experienced in that decade.

In all cases studied here the negative aspects of dependent capitalist development elicited a response from the host society. Everywhere government moved to an increasingly activist role in the economy. But the extent of the reaction and the nature of the policies adopted by the governments in question varied across the region. In general the greater the success of dependent development in raising income levels the less radical was the response. Thus Guyana which had never attracted substantial capital inflows became the locus of the most extensive government participation in the economy. In Trinidad, flushed with petro-dollars, government involvement in the economy too was extensive, but in effect confined to the role of attracting more foreign investment to the country. Jamaica's social democratic response attempted to occupy a middle position between that of Trinidad and Guyana with regard to the centrality of the private investment in the economy.

Clearly the economic performances in Jamaica and Guyana were extremely disappointing. Through the bulk of the 1970s per capita output declined, trade balances fell seriously into deficit and shortages and scarcities were rampant. What seems to have happened in both countries is that government's activism moved beyond some hard to identify, but nonetheless real, threshold which signals to private investors the existence of a hostile investment climate. It may be that Guyana would never have succeeded in attracting foreign investment in any case. If that were so the absence of foreign investment in the 1970s simply was a repetition of what went on in the past. On the other hand there is no doubt that the Manley's government articulation of democratic socialism in 1974 resulted in a precipitous decline in foreign investment in Jamaica. With this decline and in the absence of some alternative source of investment – either from domestic or alternative foreign sources – that country's previous unbalanced, but substantial, pattern of development was curtailed.

In effect what happened in both cases, though probably more purposefully in Guyana than in Jamaica, was an effort to opt out of the path of dependent development. Guyana had never really been fully integrated into world capitalism and so the shift was not traumatic. But in Jamaica the transition was difficult. For that country had become a growth center in the Caribbean. The sudden strike of capital in the 1970s represented the termination of a path of growth which had already demonstrated some measure of success.

The tragedy for the people of both countries was that no effective alternative to dependent development was implemented. With externally induced growth no longer the approach followed, there was an urgent need to initiate policies which would promote growth from within. Such an approach can be developed, but it involves a substantial reordering of programs and priorities. For above all self-reliant development necessitates emphasis on agricultural production. Where the countryside can be mobilized, the wealth necessary for autonomous expansion may be made available. If so, the possibility arises that a self-initiated development process in which benefits are widely distributed might be begun.

But precisely the problem is that in neither Jamaica nor Guyana was the enhanced role of government accompanied by a shift in attention towards agriculture. Neither George Beckford's nor C. Y. Thomas' program for the establishing of a modernized agricultural sector was essayed. As a result, the foreign private investment upon which growth in the past had been based was sharply curtailed but was not replaced by a new domestic source of dynamism. A full transition away from the model of dependent development to that of autonomous or self-reliant development did not therefore occur. As a result, poverty persisted, and may, in fact, have intensified for the people of those countries.

At root, the problem in both countries was that their governments, interested in greater autonomy, did not and probably could not successfully reorganize agriculture. Urban-based, they paid too little attention to the potential for dynamism present in the countryside. Yet agricultural transformation is essential to self-reliant growth. Thus the necessary, if not sufficient, condition for the success of an autonomous growth strategy – the existence of a government able to mobilize the rural population – was not present in either country.

In this connection mention should be made of the role of the major external power in the region, the United States of America. It has long been a matter of faith among West Indians that if a shift away from dependency were to occur they would immediately confront the hostility of the United States. Especially given the experience of Cuba and the Dominican Republic and the more recent treatment accorded the Allende government in Chile, such an anticipation is probably correct. Yet if a kind of regional fatalism is to be avoided, this prediction of North American hostility must be seen as just one more aspect – though an important one to be sure – of the difficult situation which a strategy of autonomous development must overcome.

Indeed the argument is that agriculture's claim to priority attention is stronger to the extent that opposition from abroad can be anticipated. For not only would a government in such circumstances be cut off from private sources of external capital, but recent experience suggests that it would also find official sources of funds also curtailed. There is now abundant evidence that the only means by which to escape the balance-of-payment crisis which will result from these shutoffs is to depend heavily upon an expanded agricultural sector. Thus to the extent that external hostility is predictable, an emphasis on agricultural transformation is all the more essential, and the lessons of the Cuban Revolution becomes all the more important. If output growth is the goal, policies and institutions must be designed to make certain that a conscientious and intensive work effort by the rural labor force is forthcoming.

The experience in Trinidad and Tobago is entirely different from that of Guyana and Jamaica. The former benefitted from an enormous balance-of-payments surplus situation; it is following a policy of attempting to attract foreign investors; and all of this is in conjunction with the fact it has adopted a posture distant to the Leftist regimes in the region. In consequence the United States has looked favorably upon Trinidad as a bastion of conservatism in the region.

Trinidad and Tobago therefore is well positioned to attract foreign investment. Current estimates are that it can continue to extract crude oil for the next twenty-five years. Thus it is during that time frame the replacement or replacements for oil as an income earner must be put into place.

Given the political stability demonstrated in Trinidad and Tobago in the November 1981 elections following the death of Eric Williams the country may very well become a locus of foreign investment in the region. As such, it will become a center for dependent development. One example of this is the petro-chemical industry currently under construction. With this and other industries following, it is not inconceivable to argue that Trinidad and Tobago could follow the path initiated in the region by Puerto Rico in becoming an industrialized island. To be sure there are obstacles in the way: government is inefficient and allegations of corruption abound. Infrastructure facilities are inadequate; telephone communications are unreliable and the transportation system is nearly hopelessly snarled. Despite all of this, however, it may still be the case that

Trinidad and Tobago is sufficiently hospitable and lucrative to attract large volumes of investment capital from abroad and thus experience a substantial economic expansion and structural transformation.

But the picture becomes more pessimistic when the question of the benefits of economic development is turned to and discussion centers on who is to be the likely beneficiaries of the growth process which is to occur in the country. As we saw in Chapter 3 capitalist development often has failed to advance the welfare of the population substantially. It appears likely that Trinidad will follow this pattern since current projections indicate that at no time in the foreseeable future is it likely that unemployment will be reduced substantially.

In this regard the illustration of Puerto Rico is again suggestive. That island's development strategy was undoubtedly a success in transforming and expanding its structure of output. But at no time has the growth in the demand for labor been sufficient to make a dent in its high rate of unemployment. Throughout the 1960s and 1970s unemployment has remained in excess of 10 percent and usually close to 15 percent even as mass emigration has resulted in more Puerto Ricans living off than on the island. There is nothing in Trinidad and Tobago's situation which suggests that it is better positioned to avoid this problem than was Puerto Rico. Indeed because of Puerto Rico's "Commonwealth" status precisely the opposite argument can be made. As a result the anticipation is that while development may proceed in Trinidad, the economic expansion may well fail to result in an improvement in living standards for large numbers of the country's population.

The evidence reviewed in Chapter 3 suggests that if the goal of development is to satisfy the basic needs of the people of a country a socialist is preferable to a capitalist mode of production. But the lesson to be learned from the experience of the Caribbean is that with the construction of socialism emphasis must be placed on agriculture if development is to occur, and if this emphasis does not result in expanded output development under socialism will not be viable.

Even if agriculture is accorded priority attention in the socialist mode of production the Cuban experience suggests that there will be problems finding an institutional fit to accomodate the aspirations of the people of the countryside, the goal of constructing socialist class relations and at the same time expand agricultural production. Nevertheless it is clear that with agriculture emphasized an alternative to dependent capitalist growth is feasible and that approach if successful promises a relatively substantial improvement in the standard of living of the people of the country.

The tragedy of the current situation in the Caribbean is that the one country which has experienced recent growth – Trinidad and Tobago – is following a path unlikely to benefit large numbers of its population while the "Left" regimes in Jamaica and Guyana have been unable successfully to implement an agriculturally-based autonomous development approach. Because of their urban interests, constitutencies and values, these latter governments were poorly positioned to achieve the kind of agricultural modernization their approach dictated. In both countries the "Left" governments possessed ties to the countryside which were either weak or strained. A cultural as well as a political and economic distance separated the people of the countryside from the dominant power in society. It is this breach which represented the basic difficulty in promoting agricultural advance.

It is the ability to construct relations of good will between the countryside and the city which is essential for self-reliant growth in the region to be viable. What this means is that in the future any assessment of a regime's competence with regard to elevating the conditions of life for the West Indian population should start with its ability to implement a program of transformation in agriculture. Failing that, there is not much hope. With a strong and credible presence in the countryside a regime at least has passed the first test in pursuit of a pattern of development which will have a positive impact on the lives of the people of the region.

BIBLIOGRAPHY

Adelman, Irma and Morris, Gynthia Taft Morris, *Economic Growth and Social Equity in Developing Countries* (Stanford: Stanford University Press, 1973).

Adelman, Irma and Morris, Cynthia Taft, "Growth and Improvishment in the Middle of the Nineteenth Century," *World Development*, Vol. 6, No. 3, March 1978.

Ahiram, E. "Income Distribution in Jamaica and Trinidad-Tobago," in Andic, F. M. and Mathews, T. E. eds., *Caribbean in Transition* (Rio Piedras: Institute of Caribbean Studies, 1965).

Alavi, Hamzi, "India and the Colonial Mode of Production," in Ralph Miliband and John Saville (ed.), *The Socialist Register 1975* (London: The Merlin Press, 1975).

Alavi, Hamzi, "Rural Bases of Political Power in South Asia," *Journal of Contemporary Asia* IV (4) 1974.

Alavi, Hamzi, "The State in Post-Colonial Societies," *New Left Review*, Vol. 74, July/August, 1972.

Amin, Samir, *Accumulation on a World Scale*, 2 Vols. (New York: Monthly Review Press, 1974).

Anderson, Perry, *Lineages of the Absolute State* (Atlantic Highlands Humanities Press, 1974).

Avineri, Shlomo (ed.), *Karl Marx on Colonialism and Modernization* (Garden City: Doubleday & Co. Inc. 1968).

Avineri, Shlomo, "Marx and Modernization," *Review of Politics* XXXI, 2 (April 1969).

Avineri Shlomo, *The Social and Political Thought of Karl Marx* (Cambridge: University Press, 1971).

Bagchi, A. k. "De-industrialization in India in the Nineteenth Century: Some Theoretical Implications, *Journal of Development Studies*, Vol. 12, No. 2, January 1976.

Bairoch, P. "Income Inequalities among Nations Before the Industrial Revolution and their Evolution till the 1970's, in P. Bairoch and M. Levy-Leboyer, eds., *Regional and International Disparities in Economic Development Since the Industrial Revolution* (London: Macmillan, 1981).

Banaji, Jairus, "Backward Capitalism, Primitive Accumulation and Modes of Production," *Journal of Contemporary Asia*, Vol. 3, No. 4, 1973.

Banaji, Jairus, "For a Theory of Colonial Modes of Production," *Economic and Political Weekly* (Bombay) December 23, 1972, Vol. VII, No. 52.

Banaji, Jairus, "Modes of Production in a Materialist Conception of History," *Capital and Class* 3 (1977).

Baran, Paul A., *The Political Economy of Growth* (New York: Monthly Review Press, 1957).

Barbalet, J. M., "Underdevelopment and the Colonial Economy," *Journal of Contemporary Asia*, Vol. 6, No. 2, 1976.

Beckford, George L., 'Caribbean Rural Economy," in George L. Beckford, ed., *Caribbean Economy* (Jamaica: Institute of Social and Economic Research, University of West Indies, 1975.

Beckford, George L., "Land Reform for the Betterment of Caribbean Peoples," *Proceedings of the 7th West Indies Agricultural Economics Conference* (Grand Anse, Grenada, 1972).

Bernardo, Robert, *The Theory of Moral Incentives in Cuba* (University: University of Alabama Press, 1971).

Berry, R. Albert and Cline, William R., *Agrarian Structure and Productivity in Developing Countries* (Baltimore and London: The Johns Hopkins University Press, 1979).

Best, L. "Outlines of a Model of Pure Plantation Economy," *Social and Economic Studies*, Vol. 17, No. 3, 1968.

Blaich, O. P., *Agriculture in British Guiana*, Census 1952, Vol. I, No. 1.

Bourne, Compton, "Jamaica and the International Monetary Fund: Economics of the 1978 Stabilization Program," *Studies in Rural Finance* (Agricultural Finance Program: The Ohio State University, 1980).

Brenner, Robert, "The Origin of Capitalist Development: A Critique of Neo-Smithean Marxism," *New Left Review*, #104 July/August 1977.

Cardoso, Fernando H., "Dependency in Latin America," *New Left Review* 74 (1972).

Cardoso, F. H., "Notas Sobre o Estado Atual Dependencia," in Frank Bonilla and Robert Girling, eds., *Structures of Dependency* (Nairobi, Calif.: 1973).

Cardoso, F. H., "Imperialism and Dependency in Latin America," in Frank Bonilla and Robert Girling, eds., *Structures of Dependency* (Nairobi Calif.: 1973).

Carrington E., "The Post War Political Economy of Trinidad and Tobago," and "Industrialization in Trinidad and Tobago Since 1950" in Norman Girvan and Owen Jefferson, eds., *Readings in the Political Economy of the Caribbean* (Jamaica: New World Group, 1971).

Castro Fidel, "Main Report to the Second Congress of Communist Party of Cuba," *Cuba Update*, Vol. II, No. 1, March 1981.

Clawson, Patrick, "The Internationalization of Capital and Capital Accumulation, *The Insurgent Socialist*, Spring 1977.

Cheng Ngai-Lung, "Underdevelopment and the World Capitalist System: An Evaluation of Some Recent Studies" (University of Salford, Dept. of Sociological and Political Studies, M. Sc Thesis, 1976).

Cohen, G. A., *Karl Marx's Theory of History: A Defense* (Princeton: Princeton University Press, 1978).

Cohen, Stephen F., *Burkharin and the Bolshevik Revolution*, A Political Biography 1888–1938 (New York: Alfred A. Knopf, 1973).

Conquery-Vedrovitch, Catherine, "Research on an African Mode of Production," in Martin A. Klein and G. Wesley Johnson, *Perspectives on the African Past* (Boston 1972), pp. 33–51.

Cross, Malcolm, *Urbanization and Urban Growth in the Caribbean*: An Essay on Social Change in Dependent Societies (New York: Cambridge University Press, 1978).

Cypher, James M., "The Internationalization of Capital and the Transformation of Social Formations: A Critique of the Monthly Review School," *Review of Radical Political Economics* 11:4 (Winter 1979).

"Declaration of Sophia," Address By the Leader of the People's National Congress, Prime Minister Forbes Burnham at a Special Congress to Mark the Tenth Anniversary of the PNC in Government, December 14, 1974.

Dell, Sidney, "Basic Needs or Comprehensive Development: Should the UNDP Have A Development Strategy?" *World Development*, Vol. 7, No. 3, March 1975, pp. 291–308.

Dobb, Maurice, *Studies in the Development of Capitalism* (New York: International Publishers, 1947).

Easterlin, Richard A., "Why Isn't The Whole World Developed?", Presidential Address to the Economic History Association, Boston Mass. Sept. 12, 1980, *The Journal of Economic History*, Vol. XLI, No. 1, March 1981.

Emmanuel, Arghiri, "Myths of Development versus Myths of Underdevelopment," *New Left Review*, #85, May/June 1974.

Emmanuel, Arghiri, *Unequal Exchange*, A Study of the Imperialism of Trade (New York: Monthly Review Press, 1972).

The Epica Task Force, *Jamaica: Caribbean Challenge* (Washington: Epica Task Force, 1978).

Evans, Peter, *Dependent Development: The Alliance of Multinational, State and Local Capital in Brazil* (Princeton: Princeton University Press, 1979).

"Extracts from the These on the Revolutionary Movement in Colonial and Semi-Colonial Countries adopted by the Sixth Comintern Congress," in Jane Degras (ed.), *The Communist International 1919–43*, Documents (London, New York, Toronto: Oxford University Press, 1960).

Farrell, Trevor M. A., "The Unemployment Crisis in Trinidad and Tobago: Its Current Dimensions and Some Projections to 1985," *Social and Economic Studies*, Vol. 27, No. 2, June 1978.

Fogel, Robert William and Engerman, Stanley L., *Time on the Cross: The Economics of American Negro Slavery* (Boston: Little, Brown and Company, 1974).

Foster-Carter, Aida, "From Rostow to Gunder Frank: Conflicting Paradigms in the Analysis of Underdevelopment," *World Development*, Vol. IV, No. 3 (March 1976).

Foster-Carter, Aida, "The Mode of Production Debate," *New Left Review* 107, Jan./Feb. 1978.

Foster-Carter, Aida, "Neo-Marxist Approaches to Development and Underdevelopment," *Journal of Contemporary Asia*, Vol. 111, No. 1 (1973).

Frank, Andre Gunder, *Capitalism and Underdevelopment in Latin America*, rev. ed. (New York: Monthly Review Press, 1969).

Frank, Andre Gunder, "Dependence is Dead, Long Live Dependence and the Class Struggle: An Answer to Critics," *World Development*, Vol. 5, No. 4, April 1977.

Freedman, Robert (ed.), *Marx on Economics* (New York: Harcourt, Brace and Co., 1961).

Girling, R. K., "Technology and Dependent Development in Jamaica," *Social and Economic Studies*, Vol. 25, No. 2, June 1977.

Girvan, Norman, *Foreign Capital and Economic Underdevelopment in Jamaica* (Jamaica: Institute of Social and Economic Research, University of the West Indies, 1971).

Genovese, Eugene D., *Roll, Jordan, Roll: The World the Slaves Made* (New York: Pantheon, 1975).

Genovese, Eugene D. and Fox-Genovese Elizabeth, "The Slave Economies in Political Perspective," *The Journal of American History* 66, 1 (June 1979).

Guyana, Bank of, *1976, 1979 Annual Report*.

Guyana, Bank of, *Economic Bulletin No. 9* (Georgetown October 1975).

Guyana, Government of, Ministry of Cooperatives and National Mobilization, "Growth of Cooperative Movement, 1948–1975."

Guyana, Government of, Ministry of Economic Development, *Economic Survey of Guyana 1973*.

Hanley, E., "Rice, Politics and Development in Guyana" in Oxaal I. et al. (eds.), *Beyond the Sociology of Development* (London: Routledge and Kegan Paul, 1975).

Harewood, Jack, "The Under-Utilization of Available Human Resources," in Jack Harewood ed., *Human Resources in the Commonwealth Caribbean* (Trinidad: Institute of Social and Economic Research, University of the West Indies, 1970).

Harewood, Jack, "West Indian People," in G. Beckford, ed., *Caribbean Economy: Dependence and Backwardness* (Jamaica: Institute of Social and Economic Research, University of the West Indies, 1975).

Higgins, Benjamin, "Economic Development and Cultural Change: Seamless Web or Patchwork Quilt?" in Manning Nash, ed., Essays on Economic Development and Cultural Change in Honor of Bert F. Hoselitz, *Economic Development and Cultural Change* 25, supplement, 1977.

Higman, B. W., *Slavery Population and Economy in Jamaica 1807–1834* (Cambridge: Cambridge University Press, 1976).

Hindiss, Barry and Hirst Paul Q., *Precapitalist Modes of Production* (London: Routledge and Kegan Paul, 1975).

Hopkins, A. G., *An Economic History of West Africa* (London: Longman, 1973).

Horvat, Branko, "Welfare of the Common Man in Various Countries," *World Development*, Vol. 2, No. 7, July 1974.

Hymer, S. H. and Resnick, S. A., "International Trade and Uneven Development," in Bhagwati, Jagdest, Jones, Ronald W., Mendell, Robert A. and Vanek, Jaroslav, *Trade Balance of Payments and Growth: Papers in International Economics in Honor of Charles P. Kindleberger* (Amsterdam: North-Holland Publishing Co., 1971).

International Bank For Reconstruction and Development, *World Development Report 1980* (New York: Oxford University Press, 1980).

International Bank for Reconstruction and Development, *World Tables, 2nd ed., 1980* (Baltimore and London: The John Hopkins University Press, 1980).

Jamaica, Government of, *Democratic Socialism fôr Jamaica* (Kingston: The Agency for Public Information, N.D.).

Jamaica, Government of, *Economic and Social Survey*, Jamaica 1975.

Jefferson, Owen, *The Post-War Economic Development of Jamaica* (Jamaica: Institute of Social and Economic Research, University of the West Indies, 1972).

Kamark, Andrew M., *The Tropics and Economic Development: A Provocative Inquiry into the Poverty of Nations* (Baltimore: The Johns Hopkins University Press, 1976).

Kamrany, Nake M. and Elliott, John E., *The New Economics of the Less Developed Countries* (Boulder Colorado; Westview Press, 1978).

Kiernan, V. C., "Marx and India," in Ralph Miliband and John Saville (eds.), *The Socialist Register 1967* (New York: Monthly Review Press, 1967).

Kuznets, Simon, "Modern Economic Growth: Findings and Reflections," in Simon Kuznets, *Population, Capital and Growth* (New York: W. W. Norton and Co., 1973).

Landau, Saul, Jamaica's Hot Politics," *Mother Jones*, Vol. V, No. VIII, Sept./Oct. 1980.

Latin America Regional Reports, *Caribbean*, 8 May 1981.

Lewis, Gordon K., *The Growth of the Modern West Indies* (New York: Monthly Review Press, 1968).

Lewis W. Arthur, "The Diffusion of Development" in Thomas Wilson and Andrew S. Skinner, eds., *The Market and the State, Essays in Honour of Adam Smith* (Oxford: Clarendon Press, 1976).

Lewis, W. Arthur, *The Evolution of the International Economic Order* (Princeton: Princeton University Press, 1978).

Lewis, W. Arthur, "The Industrialization of the British West Indies, *Caribbean Economic Review*, Vol. 2, 1950.

Ley, Colin, "The 'Overdeveloped' Post-Colonial State: A Reevaluation," *Review of Africa Political Economy*, No. 5.

Ley, Colin, "Underdevelopment and Dependency: Critical Note," *Journal of Contemporary Asia*, Vol. 7, No. 1, 1977.

Lipton, Michael, *Why Poor People Stay Poor: Urban Bias in World Development* (Cambridge Mass.: Harvard University Press, 1977.

MacEwan, Arthur, "Cuban Agriculture and Development" in Dharam Ghai, Azizur Rahman Khan, Eddy Lee, and Samir Radwan (eds.), *Agrarian Systems and Rural Development* (New York: Holmes and Meier Publisher Inc., 1979).

MacEwan, Arthur, *Revolution and Economic Development in Cuba* (New York: St. Martin's Press, 1981).

Macpherson, John, *Caribbean Lands: A Geography of the West Indies* (Trinidad and Jamaica: Longman Caribbean, Third Edition, 1973).

McMichael, Philip, Petras, Jones and Rhodes, Robert, "Imperalism and the Contradictions of Development," *New Left Review*, #85, May/June 1974.

Mandle, Jay R., *The Plantation Economy: Population and Economic Change in Guyana 1838–1960* (Phila.: Temple University Press, 1973).

Mandle, Jay R., "Problems of the Noncapitalist Path of Development in Guyana and Jamaica," *Politics and Society*, Vol. 7, No. 2 (1977).

Mandle, Jay R., *The Roots of Black Poverty: The Southern Plantation Economy after the Civil War* (Durham: Duke University Press, 1978).

Marx Karl, *Capital*, Critique of Political Economy (New York: Modern Library, 1906).

Mau, James A., "The Threatening Masses: Myth or Reality?" in F. M. Andic and T. C. Mathews, eds., *The Caribbean in Transition* (Rio Piedras: Institute of Caribbean Studies, University of Puerto Rico, 1965).

McFarlane, Carmen, "The Employment Situation in Overpopulated Territories in the Commonwealth Caribbean," in Jack Harewood, ed., *Human Resources in the Commonwealth Caribbean* (Trinidad: Institute of Social and Economic Research, 1970).

Melloti, Umberto, *Marx and the Third World* (Atlantic Highlands, N.J., 1977).

Mishra, Ramesh, "Technology and Social Structure in Marx's Theory: An Exporatory Analysis," *Science and Society*, Vol. XLIII, No. 2, Summer 1979.

Mohri, Kenyo, "Marx and 'Underdevelopment'", *Monthly Review*, Vol. 30, No. 1, April 1979.

Molyneux, Maxene and Halliday, Fred, "Austerity with a Human Face," *In These Times*, June 3–16, 1981.

Morawetz, David, *Twenty-Five Years of Economic Development* (Baltimore: The Johns Hopkins University Press, 1977).

Moskos, Charles C., Jr., *The Sociology of Political Independence* (Cambridge: Schenkman Publishing Company, 1967).

Myrdal, Gunnar, *Economic Theory and Underdeveloped Regions* (New York: Harper and Row, 1957).

Ohiorhenuam, John F. E., "Dependence and Non Capitalist Development in the Caribbean: Historical Necessity and Degrees of Freedom," *Science and Society*, Vol. XLIII, 4.

Palma, Gabriel, "Dependency: A Formal Theory of Underdevelopment or a Methodology for the Analysis of Concrete Situations of Underdevelopment?" *World Development*, Vol. 6, No. 7/8, July/August 1978.

Palmer, Ransford W., *Caribbean Dependence on the United States Economy* (New York: Praeger Publishers, 1979).

Patel, Surendra J., "Collective Self – Reliance of Developing Countries," *The Journal of Modern African Studies* (1975).

People's National Congress, *Constitution.*

Petras, James F., "New Perspectives on Imperialism and Social Classes in the Periphery, *Journal of Contemporary Asia*, Vol. 5, No. 3 (1975).

Petras, James F., "State Capitalism in the Third World," *Development and Change*, Winter 1977.

Portes, Alejandro, "The Sociology of National Development," *American Journal of Sociology* 82 (1), 1976, 55–85.

Premdas, Ralph R., "Elections and Political Campaigns in a Bifurcated State: The Case of Guyana," *The Journal of Inter-America Studies and World Affairs*, Vol. 14, No. 3 (1972).

Pugwash Symposium, "The Role of Self-Reliance in Alternative Strategies for Development," *World Development*, Vol. 5, No. 3 (March 1977).

Ranis, Gustav, "Development Theory at Three Quarters Century," in Manning Nash, ed., Essays on Economic Development and Cultural Change in Honor of Bert F. Hoselitz, *Economic Development and Cultural Change* 25, supplement, 1977.

Resnick, Stephen A., "The Second Path to Capitalism: A Model of International Development," *Journal of Contemporary Asia*, Vol. 3, No. 2, 1973.

Richter, Andrew S., "Multinational Corporations, Local Businessmen and the State in a Small Developing Country: A Case Study of Trinidad and Tobago" (Unpublished Ph.D. Dissertation, Yale University, 1979).

Robothom, Don, "Agrarian Relations in Jamaica," in Carl Stone and Aggrey Brown, eds., *Essays on Power and Change in Jamaica* (Jamaica: University of the West Indies, 1976).

Rodney, Walter, *How Europe Underdeveloped Africa* (London: Bogle – L'ouverturo Publications, 1972).

Rosenberg, Nathan, "The Direction of Technological Change: Inducement Mechanisms and Focusing Devices," *Economic Development and Cultural Change*, Vol. 18, No. 1, October, 1969.

Rosenberg, Nathan, "Factors Affecting the Diffusion of Technology," *Explorations in Economic History*, Fall 1972.

Rothstein, Robert, "The Political Economy of Redistribution and Self-Reliance, *World Development*, Vol. 4, No. 7 (July 1976).

Roxborough, Ian, "Dependency Theory in The Sociology of Development: Some Theoretical Problems," *Journal of Sociology of Political Science*, Vol. 1, No. 2 (Jan. 1976).

Ryan, Selwyn, "Restructuring the Trinidad Economy," in Norman Girvan and Owen Jefferson, eds., *Readings in the Political Economy of the Caribbean* (Jamaica: New World Group Ltd., 1971).

Saul, John, "The State in Post Colonial Societies – Tanzania" in Ralph Miliband and John Saville, eds., *The Socialist Register 1973* (London, 1974).

Sawer, Marian, *Marxism and the Question of the Asiatic Mode of Production* (The Hague: Martinus Nijhoff, 1977).

Sayer D., "Precapitalist Societies and Contemporary Marxist Theory," *Sociology* 11, 1 (1977) 149–53.

Senior, Olive, *The Message is Change*: A Perspective on the 1972 General Election (Kingston Jamaica: Kingston Publishers Ltd., 1972).

Silverman, Bertram, "The Great Debate in Retrospect: Economic Rationality and the Ethics of Revolution," in Bertram Silverman (ed.), *Man and Socialism in Cuba: The Great Debate* (New York: Atheneum, 1971).

Smith, Raymon T., *British Guiana* (London: Oxford University Press, 1962).

Stone, Carl, "An Appraisal of the Co-operative Process in The Jamaican Sugar Industry," *Social and Eonomic Studies*, Vol. 27, 1 (March 1978).

Taylor, John G., *From Modernization To Modes of Production*: A Critique of the Sociologies of Development and Underdevelopment (London: The Macmillan Press Ltd., 1979).

Thomas, Clive Y., *Dependence and Transformation: The Economics of the Transition to Socialism* (New York: Monthly Review Press, 1974).

Thomas, Clive Y., "Non-Capitalist Development as Theory and Practice of Decolonization and Socialist Transformation," Paper Presented to the Colloquim on Comparative Studies of Decolonization and Dependence, University of California, Berkeley, December 2, 1976.

Thompson, Edgar T., "The Plantations as a Social System," in Pan American Union, *Plantation Systems of the New World* (Washington, 1959).

Thorner, David, "Marx on India and the Asian Mode of Production," in *Contributions to Indian Sociology* (London) Vol. IX, December 1966.

Tinker, Hugh, *A New System of Slavery: The Export of Indian Labour Overseas 1830–1920* (London: Oxford University Press, 1974).

Trinidad and Tobago, Government of, *Third Five Year Plan 1969–1973*.

Trinidad and Tobago, Government of, *White Paper No. 2 on Public Sector Participation in Industry* (Trinidad: Government Printery, 1979).

Von Freghold, Michael, "The Post-Colonial State and its Tanzanian Version," *Review of African Political Economy*, No. 8.

Wagley, Charles, "Plantation America: A Culture Sphere," in Vera Rubin, ed., *Caribbean Studies: A Symposium* (Seattle: University of Washington Press, 1960).

Warren, Bill, *Imperialism: Pioneer of Capitalism* (London: NLB and Verson editions, 1980).

Warren, Bill, "Imperialism and Capitalist Industrialization," *New Left Review*, No. 81, September/October 1973.

Washington Post, August 25, 1980.

Wilkie, James W., *Statistical Abstract of Latin-America* (Los Angeles: UCLA Latin-American Center Publications, 1980).

Wood, D. Trinidad in Transition: The Years After Slavery (London: Oxford University Press, 1968).

Zamor, Jean Claude Garcia, *The Ecology of Development Administration in Jamaica, Trinidad and Tobago and Barbados* (Washington: General Secretariat, Organization of Ameican States, 1977).

Index

For Product Safety Concerns and Information please contact our EU representative GPSR@taylorandfrancis.com
Taylor & Francis Verlag GmbH, Kaufingerstraße 24, 80331 München, Germany

www.ingramcontent.com/pod-product-compliance
Ingram Content Group UK Ltd.
Pitfield, Milton Keynes, MK11 3LW, UK
UKHW022123190926
475702UK00013B/1614
9780415849135